THE WAY OF LIFE

D1607939

If there is no transcendent truth, in obedience to which man achieves his full identity, then there is no sure principle for guaranteeing just relations between people. Their self-interest as a class, group or nation would inevitably set them in opposition to one another. If one does not acknowledge transcendent truth, then the force of power takes over, and each person tends to make full use of the means at his disposal in order to impose his own interests or his own opinion, with no regard for the rights of others.

John Paul II[1]

And if it is the novelist's business to look and see what is there for everyone to see but is nonetheless not seen . . . then sooner or later he must confront the great paradox of the twentieth century: that no other time has been more life-affirming in its pronouncements, self-fulfilling, creative, autonomous, and so on—and more death-dealing in its actions. It is the century of the love of death. I am not talking just about Verdun or the Holocaust or Dresden or Hiroshima. I am talking about a subtler form of death, a death in life, of people who seem to be living lives which are good by all sociological standards and yet who somehow seem more dead than alive. Whenever you have a hundred thousand psychotherapists talking about being life-affirming and a million books about life-enrichment, you can be sure there is a lot of death around.

Walker Percy[2]

THE WAY OF LIFE
John Paul II and the Challenge of Liberal Modernity

Carson Holloway

BAYLOR UNIVERSITY PRESS

Unless otherwise stated scripture quotations are from the New Revised
Standard Version Bible, copyright 1989, Division of Christian Education
of the National Council of the Churches of Christ in the United States of
America. Used by permission. All rights reserved.

Cover Design: Pamela Poll
Cover image: Pope John Paul II. @Bernard Bisson/Sygma/Corbis. Used by
permission of Corbis Corporation.

Library of Congress Cataloging-in-Publication Data

Holloway, Carson, 1969-
  The way of life : John Paul II and the challenge of liberal modernity /
Carson Holloway.
     p. cm.
  Includes bibliographical references and index.
  ISBN 978-1-932792-96-6 (pbk. : alk. paper)
  1. Political science--Philosophy. 2. Liberalism--Philosophy. 3. Human
rights--Philosophy. 4. Catholic Church. Pope (1978-2005 : John Paul II).
Evangelium vitae. 5. Catholic Church--Doctrines--History--20th century. 6.
John Paul II, Pope, 1920-2005--Political and social views. I. Title.

  JA71.H6153 2008
  241'.697--dc22
                          2008010619

For my wife, Shari
and my daughters, Maria, Anna, Elizabeth, Catherine, and Jane

TABLE OF CONTENTS

PREFACE

Can modern society maintain its commitment to human dignity and human rights without religion? This is the live practical question with which this academic study of the thought of dead philosophers is bound up.

This book seeks to explicate the critique of liberal modernity that is, I will contend, implicit in the moral and social thought of Pope John Paul II, and in particular in his celebrated encyclical *Evangelium Vitae*, or *The Gospel of Life*. I use the term "liberal modernity" broadly to refer to certain influential intellectual and political trends of the last several centuries. That is, in this book liberal modernity refers first to the philosophic movement initiated by Thomas Hobbes and carried forward by other thinkers who have sought to organize our thinking about society and politics primarily in terms of the individual's concern with his preservation and material prosperity. In the pages to follow, however, liberal modernity is also used with reference to the contemporary political societies influenced by this philosophic movement, roughly speaking, the developed nations of the democratic West.

I hope, of course, that such a book will prove interesting to students of John Paul II's thought, of Catholic thought more generally, and of the history of political philosophy. I further hope, however, that the book will find a broader audience of thoughtful citizens interested in reflecting on the contribution that religious thought can make to the maintenance of the decent and just society to which all people of good will aspire. This appeal to a broader audience and a more practical concern is in keeping with the subject matter examined here. John Paul II was not only a philosopher but also a pastor and leader. He did not intend his works—and certainly not his papal encyclicals—to be of merely academic interest, but sought by them to identify what he took to be grave weaknesses in our civilization's public philosophy, weaknesses to which he believed the intellectual tradition to which he belonged could provide the necessary remedy.

Liberal modernity is characterized by a turning away from the fundamental concerns of premodern political thought. More specifically, liberal modernity's preoccupation with the individual's worldly interest in comfortable self-preservation goes hand in hand with a rejection of the ancient and medieval belief that our thinking about society and politics should be oriented toward a Supreme Good that somehow transcends the world yet can nevertheless be approached through a life of moral nobility. Put simply, liberal modernity rejects the lofty pursuit of virtue in favor of a more mundane pursuit of material security and satisfaction.

This seemed like a good idea at the time. The minds of Hobbes and his successors had been deeply impressed by the havoc wreaked by the religious wars of the sixteenth and seventeenth centuries, and they accordingly concluded that European man's preoccupation with the Truth about the Supreme Good, and his related concern with the well-being of his own and his neighbor's soul, was necessarily a source of bitter and unresolvable conflict and, as such, something we could do better without. It also seems like a good idea to many people today. Especially since the terrorist attacks of September 11, 2001, many American and European intellectuals have argued that the world would be better off without religion, the otherworldly high-mindedness of which, they suggest, leads paradoxically but inevitably to the most brutal acts of cruelty.

In contrast, the thought of John Paul II suggests that liberal modernity, whatever the humane intentions of its original architects and contemporary proponents, is fundamentally flawed, for its philosophic presuppositions cannot sustain its laudable commitment to human dignity and human rights. For John Paul II, the "low but solid ground" on which the moderns were said to have built turns out to be low but not-so-solid.[3] Those who seek to erect human community on the basis of an individual self-interest unconcerned with humanity's ultimate and highest end turn out to have established society upon a kind of moral swamp in which men are apt to sink to increasing depths of injustice, tyranny, and misery. Whether this diagnosis is correct is for the open-minded reader to judge, but I do not think it is one the thoughtful and earnest citizen can ignore.

ACKNOWLEDGMENTS

This book could not have been written without the support of many people and institutions to whom I am happy to express my gratitude.

I would like, first, to thank Baylor University Press for publishing this book, and in particular its director, Carey Newman, for his encouragement and help in bringing the project to completion. I am also grateful to Baylor's anonymous reviewers for their helpful suggestions.

A good portion of the research for the book was done during the 2005–2006 academic year, when I was a William E. Simon Visiting Fellow in Religion and Public Life in the James Madison Program in American Ideals and Institutions at Princeton University. I wish to thank the Madison Program for supporting my work and the Simon Foundation for supporting the fellowship. In addition, I must express my deep gratitude to Robby George, the Madison Program's director, and Brad Wilson, its associate director, for their support, encouragement, and friendship, and in general for running an institution with which it was an honor to be associated and in which it was a joy to participate. I am also profoundly grateful to the other Madison fellows in residence during the 2005–2006 year: Matt Holland, Alan Gibson, Brad Watson, Paul Moreno, and Cathy McCauliff. All helped me by providing wise advice, delightful and enlightening conversation, and generous friendship. My year of companionship with them is a blessing I will never forget. During my stay at Princeton I was also blessed with a number of other friendships that made the year that much more enjoyable and beneficial. Here I would mention, with many thanks and much affection, Fr. Marty Miller, David Oakley, Luis Tellez, Jim Snow, and Vince West.

I am also grateful to the University of Nebraska at Omaha—especially to Shelton Hendricks, Dean of the College of Arts and Sciences—for supporting my Madison fellowship. In addition, I want to thank Gary Glenn and Thomas Lindsay for encouraging me to pursue this project and for recommending me to the Madison Program. Finally, I would like to thank John and Cara Ayers, Dave and Jynell Brockhaus, and John and Eileen Safranek for the friendship they have shown me and my family.

This book is dedicated, with my love, to my wife, Shari, and our daughters, Maria, Anna, Elizabeth, Catherine, and Jane. My debt to them is incalculable.

Any merit this book might possess could not have been achieved without the support of the people acknowledged here. Any defects in it are strictly my own.

Chapter 1

INTRODUCTION

When Pope John Paul II died in the spring of 2005, he left behind a world struck with wonder.

The world wondered, in the first place, at the remarkable conclusion of a remarkable life. Karol Wojtyła had witnessed, in some cases from the position of a key actor, the great events of a momentous century, yet he had lived to see and to celebrate the dawn of a new century and a new millennium. He had come to Rome as something new and strange, the first non-Italian pope in centuries and the first Polish pope ever, yet he departed as something so familiar as to seem almost permanent: he had served so long, and had with such confidence not only occupied but transformed his office, that by the time of his death it was difficult for most people to remember or imagine another pope. He had been elevated to the Chair of Peter at the age of fifty-eight, young by the standard of his office and impressive in his vigor and athleticism. He departed a quarter-century later, old by any standard, bent and slowed by age, injury, and illness. Yet, as he summoned all his energy to fulfill the heavy burdens of his office until the end, his love of life seemed as evident in his decline as in his prime.

His passing, however, provoked not only wonder *at* but also wonder *about* John Paul II. The efforts of public commentators to sum up his life raised the question of his significance by bringing to light disputes about it. As one writer noted, much of the commentary tended to present the pope as a paradoxical figure, a man of contradictions.[1] Perhaps it is not surprising, then, that much of the commentary was itself contradictory, made up of different currents of opinion offering very different understandings of John Paul II. To be sure, no one disputed the fact of his significance. Even his harshest critics admitted that he must be considered one of the major figures of the twentieth century. The question concerned, rather, the precise character of his significance. What did he mean to the world in which he lived, thought, and acted?

In seeking John Paul II's significance one can, of course, point to the rather obviously remarkable aspects of his public life. Reigning for more than twenty-six years, his was one of the longest papacies in history. Only Pius IX and Peter himself served longer. By traveling more frequently and more widely than any of his predecessors, and by taking enthusiastic advantage of modern communications, he was "indisputably, the most visible pope in history" and perhaps "the most visible human being in history."[2] Nevertheless, such facts, impressive though they may be, do little to reveal the core of his importance. After all, few would contend that he was merely a time-serving globe-trotter. We might look to his active role in international politics and diplomacy, and in particular his part in the collapse of European communism. Here we would undoubtedly touch upon a key aspect of John Paul II's substantive importance.[3] Yet we would not do much to resolve the question of his significance, because his contribution to the anticommunist cause is not in dispute. It is rather, again, something admitted even by his detractors, and thus something more wondered *at* than *about.*

The question raised in the wake of John Paul II's death—or at least one important question, the one to which this study is addressed—is, then, the question of his significance for the modern West, or for the liberal democracies of the developed world. What was the pope's relationship to modernity? Put crudely, was he its friend or foe? This is the question implicit in the differing views put forward in the various commentaries on his life. The intellectual organs of establishment liberalism tended to present John Paul II as modernity's enemy. Thus, for example, *The New York Times* editorial noting the pope's passing presented him as "a man who used the tools of modernity to struggle against the modern world."[4] Similarly, Peter J. Boyle's *New Yorker* piece on the elevation of Joseph Ratzinger to the papacy held that the newly elected Benedict XVI "clearly shares the view of his friend and predecessor that the Church must stand against modernity."[5] In contrast, the sources of mainstream conservative opinion tended implicitly or explicitly to reject such a charge. Writing in the *Weekly Standard*, Joseph Bottum portrayed the pope not as opposed to but as somehow larger than modernity: John Paul II, he contended, "never saw his medievalism as reactionary anti-modernism, or his modernism as enlightened anti-medievalism."[6] Likewise, in a *Wall Street Journal* opinion piece, papal biographer George Weigel took care to distinguish John Paul II from other "truly 'conservative' critics of late modernity" in that the Pope's "counter-proposal was not a rollback" of modernity but a biblical humanism based on the understanding of human beings as created in God's image and likeness.[7] Here Weigel seemed to be responding not only to the discourse brought forth by the Pope's death but also to the earlier claim, made by historian Conor Cruise O'Brien (and noted by Weigel in the opening pages of his biography), that John Paul II sought a "Repeal of the Enlightenment."[8] Although much more strident—because it was not made in the context of the Pope's passing—O'Brien's suggestion seems nevertheless to capture the substance of the view expressed by liberals and denied by conservatives in the spring of 2005—namely, that the Pope was an enemy of modernity.

This book seeks to shed light on this dispute by examining the relationship of John Paul II's thought to liberal modernity—that tradition of theory and practice aiming to organize political life around the rights of the individual understood as a primarily self-interested being.[9] Thus the following chapters examine the political thought of Thomas Hobbes, John Locke, David Hume, the American founding, as well as Tocqueville's account of modern democracy, in light of John Paul II's argument in his celebrated 1995 encyclical letter, *Evangelium Vitae*. At first glance, such an undertaking might seem unusual. Why, one might ask, should one so pair the pope's thought with this predominantly Anglo-American tradition of reflection? After all, his voluminous writings contain scant mention of such figures. Accordingly, most studies of his thought have focused on its well-known sources, either the Thomism he learned as a seminarian, the mysticism of Saint John of the Cross, or the more recent continental philosophy—and particularly the phenomenology—that John Paul II sought to appropriate to his purposes.[10] The pairing presented here, however, is appropriate to this book's task, which is not so much to explore the philosophic influences on John Paul II's social thought as to discover that thought's bearing in relation to liberal modernity. My effort has been to understand the aforementioned body of modern thought, which has done so much to shape the contemporary West, in light of the pope's most well-known critique of the contemporary West.

On the other hand, one might ask why I draw so heavily on *Evangelium Vitae*. John Paul II, after all, was a remarkably prolific author, producing a large number of official Church documents as well as a variety of his own philosophic and theological reflections dating back to his time as a young professor and priest in Poland. Nevertheless, it is surely reasonable to treat *Evangelium Vitae* as offering the most mature statement of John Paul II's view of the politics and culture of the modern West—a topic that could not so powerfully occupy his attention before he became pope, or even during the first half of his pontificate, a period during which he was concerned primarily with the problem of communism. In any case, *Evangelium Vitae* is clearly the single work that is both most relevant to the question at issue here—John Paul II's posture toward the liberal modernity characteristic of the developed West—and, at the same time, to be ranked without question among his most lastingly important encyclicals. Accordingly, while I do draw upon other papal texts when they illuminate the issues at hand, the account that follows takes as its primary point of departure John Paul II's argument in *Evangelium Vitae*.

As the subsequent chapters will reveal, this investigation leads to an understanding of John Paul II's position that differs from both the liberal and the conservative views mentioned before, but that nonetheless recognizes that both point in different ways to the complex truth concerning the pope's assessment of liberal modernity. On the one hand, I find that John Paul II's critique of liberal modernity is deeper than is commonly understood. It is in fact a radical critique, one that goes to the very philosophic roots of liberal modernity and finds there serious theoretical deficiencies. To that extent it is understandable that some liberal observers would come to the conclusion that he is an enemy of modernity. On the other hand, it is nevertheless also true, as his conservative defenders hold, that John Paul II did not understand himself as an opponent of modernity, and that his critique, though profound, is tempered by a genuine appreciation for modernity's achievements and sympathy for its aspirations. Indeed, even his critique itself is, as we shall see, offered in the spirit of a kind of friendship, a spirit similar to that animating Tocqueville's *Democracy in America*. For Tocqueville's critique of modern democracy and John Paul II's critique of liberal modernity have the same aim in view: not rejection, but improvement. Thus it would be reasonable for liberal modernity to attend to the pope's thought, receiving it not as the attack of an embittered enemy but as the criticism of a candid friend.

Chapter 2

THE GOSPEL OF LIFE
AND THE CULTURE OF DEATH

Evangelium Vitae, or *The Gospel of Life*, is probably the most famous of John Paul II's many encyclicals. By directly and decisively addressing two highly controversial issues of widespread interest—abortion and euthanasia—the document generated an extraordinary amount of comment beyond the Catholic community and thus achieved a public prominence that is unusual for papal pronouncements. Moreover, in naming the phenomenon he discerned and condemned, John Paul II introduced to the wider culture an expression of remarkable durability: the term "culture of death" has found a lasting place in our public discourse and is now commonly invoked even by non-Catholic politicians and commentators, especially those concerned with what they perceive as the threats to human life posed by modern medicine and biotechnology.[1] But what is "the culture of death"? To raise this question is to suggest that John Paul II's most famous encyclical, as well as his most celebrated trope, are more commonly recognized than profoundly understood.[2]

Most obviously, "the culture of death" refers to abortion and euthanasia. In *Evangelium Vitae* John Paul II reiterates the traditional Catholic teaching that "the direct and voluntary killing of an innocent human being is always gravely immoral," that it "can never be licit either as an end in itself or as a means to a good end," and that no human authority can

7

"legitimately recommend or permit such an action."³ He then proceeds explicitly to condemn abortion, euthanasia, and suicide as specific cases of the immoral taking of innocent human life.⁴ Moreover, he reaffirms these principles with the full authority of the Church's teaching office.⁵

Mere condemnation of these particular phenomena, however, is surely not the pope's primary purpose. After all, insofar as these condemnations represent the restatement of a teaching that was already well established and well known, *Evangelium Vitae*'s unique contribution must lie elsewhere. The surface organization of the encyclical suggests as much: its definitive statements on the morality of murder, abortion, euthanasia, and suicide require only three sections out of a total of hundred and five.

The pope's more philosophic aims come to light in his discussion of the Bible's account of the first murder, the story of Cain and Abel in the book of Genesis. In response to Cain's fratricide, the Lord poses to him a question, "What have you done?"—a question that invites him to go beyond the fact of the crime itself to face "the gravity of the motives which occasioned it and the consequences that result from it."⁶ This question, John Paul II insists, is addressed also to us today, not only to make us realize the seriousness of contemporary attacks on human life, but also to invite us to "discover what causes these attacks and feeds them" and to "ponder seriously the consequences which derive from these attacks for the existence of individuals and peoples."⁷ *Evangelium Vitae*'s primary purpose, then, is not merely to invoke authority in order to condemn contemporary attacks on human life, but to invoke reason in order to understand their meaning, to grasp why these attacks occur and what they portend.

The pope acknowledges what we might call the proximate and ultimate causes of such actions: on the one hand, the free choice of the will, sometimes influenced by difficult material circumstances, and, on the other hand, the wound original sin has inflicted on human nature, which is now somewhat inclined to evil.⁸ The core of the encyclical's argument, however, is directed instead to a kind of intermediate cause—not to these perennial and in some sense natural aspects of the human condition, but to a new climate of thought, the unwholesome fruit of a misunderstanding of man and his obligations, that believes that attacks on innocent human life are in some cases permissible. *Evangelium Vitae*, then, is addressed not just to the problem "of the destruction of so many human lives still to be born or in their final stage," but to a darkening of the conscience that makes it "increasingly difficult to distinguish between good and evil in what concerns the basic value of human life," to a "problem which exists at the cultural, social and political level": an increasing "tendency" to understand certain attacks on innocent life "as legitimate expressions of individual freedom, to be acknowledged and protected as actual rights."[9] The "culture of death" is, after all, a *culture*. It is not merely an aggregation of certain actions, but includes a whole system of thought to which today those actions are bound: the moral and intellectual causes that seem to justify them, and, in turn, the moral, intellectual, and political consequences that follow from such justifications. This is what we must seek if we wish to understand what John Paul II means by the culture of death.

Death, however, appears to be a kind of negation or denial. It would therefore seem that it can be best understood in light of that which it negates or denies.[10] To understand the culture of death we must first understand the gospel of life.

THE GOSPEL OF LIFE

What is life, on the Christian understanding? Its meaning is clearly not exhausted by mere biological existence. Although the pope is certainly concerned to defend the bodily life of human beings against mortal attacks, he begins *Evangelium Vitae* by asserting the Christian understanding of life in its highest, most spiritual sense. Thus in the "Introduction" to the encyclical, indeed in its very first section, John Paul II draws our attention to the "heart" of Jesus' "redemptive mission," which is revealed in his claim to have come that human beings "may have life, and have it abundantly." This passage from the Gospel of John, the pope contends, refers to "that 'new' and 'eternal' life which consists in communion with the Father. . . . It is precisely in this 'life' that all the aspects and stages of human life achieve their full significance."[11] Human life, it seems, cannot be properly understood—and, presumably, properly valued and protected—except in the light of the life of God and man's participation in it.

What light does the divine life shed on the life of man? We might note in the first place that man is a creature. As such he belongs to his creator, and his life is not his to dispose of according to his own will or whim. Human life is "inviolable," John Paul II argues, "as something which does not belong" to man, "because it is the gift and property of God the Creator and Father." "Man's life is from God" and "is his gift," and "God therefore is the sole Lord of this life: man cannot do with it as he wills."[12]

Such considerations alone, however, do not adequately ground the inviolability of human life. After all, there are other living beings that owe their origin to God's creative power, and yet that man may guiltlessly, in some cases at least, destroy: it is innocent *human* life that is inviolable, not innocent animal life. Thus the pope emphasizes not only the creatureliness of man's nature, but also its unique dignity. Man is a creature like any other animal, yet he is unlike all the rest in that he alone is created in the "image" and "likeness" of God himself. Thus "man, although formed from the dust of the earth, is a manifestation of God in the world, a sign of his presence, a trace of his glory." Man possesses "a sublime dignity, based on the intimate bond which unites him to his Creator: in man there shines forth a reflection of God himself." This unique dignity is based especially upon man's unique possession of certain capacities that manifest a power like God's own. Thus John Paul II speaks of the divine image as being manifested in "those spiritual faculties which are distinctively human, such as reason, discernment between good and evil, and free will."[13]

Man's dignity resides not merely in these capacities, however, but in the use to which they are made to be put. The pope therefore points to the loftiness of the human vocation as the basis of the dignity and inviolability of human life. By the exercise of his distinctive faculties of reason and free will, man "alone, among all visible creatures, is 'capable of knowing and loving his Creator.'" Accordingly, the "life which God bestows upon man is much more than existence in time" but is "a drive toward the fullness of life."[14] That is, man is called, through the proper exercise of his reason and will, to eternal life—not only in the sense of life after bodily death, but also in the sense of participating, in this present life, in the life of the eternal God by knowing and loving him.

Thus "eternal life" is to know God, and the life that Jesus came to give to men "consists of being begotten of God and sharing in the fullness of his love."[15]

Moreover, it is in this communion with God in knowledge and love that man achieves his true and fullest happiness. "Because he is made by God and bears within himself an indelible imprint of God, man is naturally drawn to God," John Paul II contends, quoting with approval the words of Saint Augustine: "You have made us for yourself, O Lord, and our hearts are restless until they rest in you."[16] Thus when human beings seek that eternal life that is "full participation in the life of the 'Eternal One,'" they obey the "deepest yearnings of the heart" for "God himself, the definitive goal and fulfillment of every person."[17] Again, it is this elevated happiness of which man is capable, the "loftiness" of his "supernatural vocation," that "reveals the greatness and inestimable value" even of temporal life, which is, to be sure, not the ultimate reality, but still a "sacred reality."[18] Thus the "dignity of this life is linked not only to its beginning, to the fact that it comes from God, but also to its final end, to its destiny of fellowship with God in knowledge and love of him."[19]

LAW, LOVE, AND LIFE

According to John Paul II, this happy union with God is achieved through obedience to his law. Jesus taught that those who "would enter life" must keep the commandments. "The teacher," the pope notes, "is speaking about eternal life, that is, a sharing in the life of God himself. This life is attained through observance of the Lord's commandments, including the commandment 'You shall not kill.'"[20] Here John Paul II follows up the teaching of his earlier encyclical on moral theology, *Veritatis Splendor*, in which he contends that God ordered man toward his final end through the law "inscribed on his heart," the "natural law." This law is reflected in the Decalogue, and hence the Ten Commandments "teach us man's true humanity," and man, by "performing morally good acts," "strengthens, develops, and consolidates within himself his likeness to God."[21]

On this understanding, one necessarily harms *oneself* by violating God's law and destroying innocent human life. The prohibition of murder, like all the "negative moral precepts," is absolute and inviolable, always and everywhere, because such action "is radically incompatible with the love of God and the dignity of the person created in his image." Thus one who murders does violence not just to the bodily life of another, but also to his own essential humanity. It is in this light that John Paul II reiterates, in *Evangelium Vitae*, the teaching of the Second Vatican Council that assaults on innocent human life "do more harm to those who practice them than to those who suffer from the injury."[22]

Indeed, insofar as God's law is a path of life, adherence to it is the source of true human fulfillment and happiness. Not only is violation of God's law not compatible with the human good, but following it is itself the human good.[23] Man's obedience to God's law is not, John Paul argues in *Veritatis Splendor*, "a heteronomy," not, that is, an imposition of moral principles "extraneous to man" and "unrelated to his good." Law-abidingness in this sense "would be nothing but a form of alienation, contrary to the divine wisdom and to the dignity of the human person."[24] The good commanded by God's law "is not added to life as a burden which weighs on it," but is itself "the very purpose of life."[25] That is, morality ultimately looks to "the absolute Good which attracts us and beckons us," to "God who is the origin and goal of man's life."[26] Moral actions "express the voluntary ordering of the person towards his ultimate end: God himself, the supreme good in whom he finds full and perfect happiness."[27] It is in light of this understanding that John Paul can speak, in *Familiaris Consortio*, of "the primacy of moral values," which are "the values of the human person as such" and therefore are bound up with "the ultimate meaning of life." On this view, the moral order "reveals and sets forth the plan of God the Creator," and accordingly "cannot be something that harms man." Rather, the moral order answers "the deepest demands of the human being created by God" and serves the person's "full humanity with the delicate and binding love whereby God Himself inspires, sustains and guides every creature towards its happiness."[28]

Of course, the moral order of which John Paul II speaks does more than merely forbid evil actions, and the happiness that flows from obedience to it requires more than merely leaving others alone. The negative moral precepts indicate the minimum of respect that one must give to other human beings, but, as Augustine remarks, observance of such precepts is only "the beginning of freedom, not perfect freedom."[29] With regard to the issues at the center of *Evangelium Vitae*, the pope points out that God's law not only forbids killing but also requires that we take positive steps to protect human life. Thus the Old Testament law not only prohibited murder, but also "dealt with protecting and defending life when it was weak and threatened: in the case of foreigners, widows, orphans, the sick and poor in general, including children in the womb." Indeed, the requirements of morality go even further, demanding more than some minimally decent positive solicitude for the lives of others. The law given in the Old Testament "culminates in the positive commandment which obliges us to be responsible for our neighbor as for ourselves: 'You shall love your neighbor as yourself.'"[30]

Ultimately, the pope argues, the pinnacle and fulfillment of the love required by the moral law, through which man realizes his true humanity, is exemplified by Christ's sacrifice of his own life for others. "Christ's blood reveals to man that his greatness, and therefore his vocation, consists in the sincere gift of self." Human beings are called to follow Christ in such sacrifice, for temporal life is given to us in order "to be brought to perfection in love and in the gift of ourselves to God and to our brothers and sisters."[31] We find, then, in the Cross the "fulfillment and the complete revelation of the Gospel of life," which culminates in the paradox of Christianity: the way to life is through death to self. Whoever loses his life will find it, and whoever saves his life will lose it.[32]

The rigorous, not to say daunting, demands of Christian morality do not, however, alter, for the pope, its status as the source of genuine human happiness. By coming not to be served but to serve, by laying down his life, "Jesus proclaims that life finds its center, its meaning, and its fulfillment when it is given up." The "fundamental expression" of the law perfected in the New Testament, which follows "the example of the Lord who gave his life for his friends," is "the gift of self in love for one's brothers and sisters." This, the pope affirms, "is the law of freedom, joy, and blessedness."[33]

This account of self-sacrifice as self-fulfillment arises from John Paul II's Christian anthropology. Once again, God created man in his own image and likeness. Yet God is love, and therefore the identity and destiny of the being made in his image and likeness cannot be grasped apart from love. The pope contends in *Familiaris Consortio* that as God called man into being "*through love*, He called him at the same time *for love*." "God is love," is a "personal loving communion" among three persons sharing the same divine nature. Thus by creating man in his image, God made love "the fundamental and innate vocation of every human being."[34]

THE GOSPEL OF LIFE AND REVELATION AND REASON

It might seem that the teaching of *Evangelium Vitae* depends entirely upon revealed Christian doctrine. The very title of the encyclical, "The Gospel of Life," seems to imply revelation, and in fact the first sentence of the work speaks of this gospel of life as being "at the heart of Jesus' message."[35] Other formulations reinforce this impression. For example, at one point John Paul II remarks as follows: "*For the Christian*" the new law "involves an absolute imperative to respect, love and promote the life of *every brother and sister*, in accordance with the requirements of God's bountiful law in Jesus Christ. 'He laid down his life for us; and we ought to lay down our lives *for the brethren*' (1 Jn. 3:16)."[36] Such a passage, at least taken in isolation, could be read to suggest that the gospel of life applies only to Christians, and even only in their dealings with their brothers and sisters in the faith.

Other passages, however, indicate that this is not the pope's intention. Rather, taken as a whole, his argument suggests that while the moral teaching of the encyclical admittedly receives support from Christian faith, it is nonetheless also accessible somehow to human reason. Thus, although the title refers to the "gospel" and hence calls revelation to mind, the opening salutation indicates that the pope's arguments are nonetheless addressed not only to believers but "to all people of good will." An appreciation for the "sacredness" and "inviolability" of life, John Paul II suggests, is imprinted on man's very nature. It is "written from the beginning in man's heart, in his conscience," which perceives life "as something which does not belong to him, because it is the property and gift of God the Creator and Father." Thus the "Gospel of life is not for believers alone" but for "everyone," because while life "has a sacred and religious value," that value "is one which every human being can grasp by the light of reason."[37]

Even the loftiest elements of the gospel of life are presented by John Paul II as accessible to reason. "The commandment 'You shall not kill,'" he contends, "even in its more positive aspects of respecting, loving and promoting human life, is binding on every individual human being." For this command "resounds in the moral conscience of everyone as an irrepressible echo of the original covenant of God the Creator with mankind. It can be recognized by everyone through the light of reason and it can be observed thanks to the mysterious working of the Spirit who, blowing where he wills, comes to and involves every person living in the world."[38] Elsewhere, the pope suggests that it is from the conscience that, despite the deforming influences of the culture of death, a "new journey of love, openness and service to life can begin."[39]

It may seem strange that the most demanding elements of Christian morality are thought by the pope to be accessible to reason. This view, however, can perhaps be understood as a reflection of John Paul's understanding of the relationship of Christian revelation to human nature. That revelation, like the moral law discussed earlier, is no "heteronomy," is not some doctrine alien to man's being and happiness. On the contrary, the pope contends that the gospel of life, while in some sense "received from the Lord" as revelation, nonetheless "has a profound and persuasive echo in the heart of every person—believer or nonbeliever alike—because it marvelously fulfills all the heart's expectations while infinitely surpassing them."[40] Thus the Christian moral teaching, once revealed, shows itself as a kind of key to man's deepest and highest longings, a clarification and perfection of his somewhat inchoate but always present and recognizable inclination towards nobility and greatness. Or, as John Paul II suggests in *Centesimus Annus*, man is by nature a religious being, and Christ is "the existentially adequate response to the desire in every human heart for goodness, truth and life."[41] On John Paul's view, then, even when Christian morality is lived to its fullest and most demanding extreme, it still resonates with human nature. Hence his remark in *Fides et Ratio* that the "martyrs," those who have died for the faith, "stir in us a profound trust because they give voice to what we already feel and they declare what we would like to have the strength to express."[42]

THE SUPREME GOOD AND THE INVIOLABILITY OF LIFE

John Paul II sums up the consequences of the gospel of life as follows:

> [H]uman life, as a gift from God, is sacred and inviolable. For this
> reason procured abortion and euthanasia are absolutely unacceptable.
> Not only must human life not be taken, but it must be protected with
> loving concern. The meaning of life is found in giving and receiving
> love, and in this light human sexuality and procreation reach their
> true and full significance. Love also gives meaning to suffering and
> death; despite the mystery which surrounds them, they can become
> saving events.[43]

According to John Paul II's teaching, the taking of innocent human
life is unconditionally prohibited. Finally, however, the gospel of life
protects human life not only by a flat prohibition of homicide, but by
identifying a supreme good—union with God through moral action and,
ultimately, gift of self—worthy of man's total commitment, and in light
of which commitment the motives to homicide tend to dissipate.[44]

Thus those who fully embrace the pope's teaching will not be
tempted to destroy others—for example, the unborn, the aged, or the
sick—whose existence threatens their material interests, because they
will realize that the satisfactions to be gained from serving those in need
far outweigh the satisfactions that arise from unimpeded material comfort. Accordingly, the pope calls upon his readers to build up a culture
of life by means of "daily gestures of openness, sacrifice and unselfish
care" for the weakest and most needy, yet at the same time reminds them
that it is precisely through such self-sacrifice that they will find "true
freedom, peace and happiness."[45]

Similarly, those who suffer pain and sickness will not be tempted
to self-destruction, for they will realize that the dignity and worthi-
ness of their lives comes not from freedom from pain but the ability to
love. Hence the pope's praise for the "courage and serenity" of those
who endure patiently the burden of "serious disabilities," whose heroism
"bears eloquent witness to what gives authentic value to life, and makes
it, even in difficult conditions, something precious for them and for others."[46] It is in this context that we can understand his judgment that

suicide involves not only a "rejection" of obligations to others, but even of "love of self."[47] While some might contend that suicide can be undertaken precisely out of self-love—as when, for example, pain or physical limitations make one's own life seem unendurable—John Paul II's teaching indicates that this is possible only on the basis of a mistaken self-love informed by an impoverished understanding of what makes life lovable. Suicide may end bodily pain, but it does so at the cost of the opportunity to continue the gift of self in this life, even under difficult circumstances. Suicide chosen on such supposedly humane grounds implicitly prefers material comfort to moral virtue, thus embraces a lesser good in preference to a greater, and thus represents a failure of genuine self-love.

THE CULTURE OF DEATH

As the gospel of life is understood in a broad sense, so may be the culture of death. That is, if the gospel of life is defined by acknowledgment of God as the supreme good for man, union with whom is achieved through adherence to the moral law, and ultimately through the gift of self, then in some sense the culture of death is the rejection of these principles. Put more simply, if the culture of life is a culture of love, then the culture of death is constituted by a denial of love. Thus the pope quotes with approval from the *Didache*, which associates "the way of death" not only with homicide but also with failure to love: "The way of death is this: . . . they show no compassion for the poor, they do not suffer with the suffering, they do not acknowledge their Creator, they kill their children and by abortion cause God's creatures to perish; they drive away the needy, oppress the suffering, they are advocates of the rich and unjust judges of the poor; they are filled with every sin."[48]

Moreover, *Evangelium Vitae* suggests that the culture of death in the broad sense leads inevitably to the culture of death in the more obvious sense. That is, denial of God and love leads to an embrace of abortion, euthanasia, and suicide. Contemporary readers, even those inclined to agree with John Paul's condemnations of such actions, may be tempted to resist such a connection. It will perhaps seem disproportionate to suggest that we cannot draw back from such evils without going so far as to embrace a culture of generous self-sacrifice. Can we not instead accommodate the primacy of individual self-interest—seemingly a central tenet of the modern, secular world in which we must live—while still setting decent limits on it? After all, to decline to love my neighbor is not the same as to want to kill him. Surely I can just leave him alone. Indeed, contemporary societies seem committed to establishing themselves on precisely this middle ground. That is, modern men want to set aside the controversial question of the supreme good and yet still live peaceably, decently, and even humanely with their fellows. If they are uninterested in, or even put off by, John Paul II's rather demanding call to love, they nevertheless desire to affirm some kind of justice and even compassion.

Nevertheless, John Paul II's argument points insistently to a link between the abandonment of love and the culture of death. In one passage, the pope contends that a "root" of the denial of the right to life is an individualistic understanding of freedom that "gives no place to solidarity, to openness to others and service of them." When love is denied, it seems, all that remains is the primacy of self-interest, such that freedom then must degenerate from freedom to serve into the "freedom of 'the strong' against the weak who have no choice but to submit." Therefore the pope contrasts the truths that "God entrusts us to one another" and that freedom is to be used for "the gift of self" with the individualism of the murderer Cain, manifested in his question to God: "Am I my brother's keeper?" This relationship between refusal to love, on the one hand, and descent into homicide, on the other, is perhaps most strikingly suggested in John Paul's choice of a quotation from the first letter of John: "For this is the message which you have heard from the beginning, that we should love one another, and not be like Cain who was of the evil one and murdered his brother."[49] Modern man seems to want human dignity without human greatness, respect for basic rights without a vocation to service in the quest for the supreme good. That is, he wants neither love nor murder but simple decency and security. John Paul II, however, suggests that no such middle ground is possible.

In *Evangelium Vitae*, John Paul II sketches an account of how the denial of love leads to the affirmation of abortion, suicide, and euthanasia. The deepest root of the "culture of death," he suggests, can be found in "the heart of the tragedy being experienced by modern man: the eclipse of the sense of God and man, typical of a social and cultural climate dominated by secularism."[50] When "God is forgotten," the pope contends, man himself "grows unintelligible." When "the sense of God is lost, the sense of man is also threatened and poisoned." Specifically, when man turns from God, he loses the sense of his own "dignity," of the "transcendent" and "sacred" character of his own life.[51] That transcendent dignity arises, on John Paul II's account, from the loftiness of man's vocation or calling: to achieve union with God, the absolute good, through adherence to the moral law and ultimately through the gift of self.[52]

The loss of God as the absolute good, the pope suggests, leads to the loss of morality as absolutely obligatory. "Dechristianization," he argues in *Veritatis Splendor* results in "an eclipse of fundamental principles and ethical values" and thus gives rise to "subjectivism" and "relativism," finally leading "of necessity" to a "decline or obscuring of the moral sense." Again, he indicates elsewhere in the same encyclical that the loss of "the sense of the transcendent" leads to "a radically subjectivistic conception of moral judgment."[53] Without God as the supreme good, it seems, human beings cannot maintain an understanding of morality as objectively true and absolutely binding. Yet, as the pope argues in *Evangelium Vitae*, once "objective and universal truth" is rejected, the "person ends up by no longer taking as the sole point of reference for his own choices the truth about good and evil, but only his subjective and changeable opinion, or, indeed, his selfish interest and whim."[54] In such circumstances, "it becomes impossible to establish personal rights on a firm and rational basis," and the right to life of the weak and vulnerable will not be thought inviolable but somehow negotiable. Thus the denial of the gospel of life in its fullness, by removing the grounds on which the prohibition on homicide might be thought absolute, opens the door to the possible permissibility of the destruction of some innocent human lives. Yet it is clear that in such circumstances our eyes will turn first to those lives whose value is obscured by imperfection or deficiency: the unborn, the aged, the debilitated.

More than that, the denial of God as man's final end for which he must strive through love undermines the motives for a strict respect for the right to life. As noted before, on John Paul II's explication of the gospel of life, the moral law, including the prohibition on murder, is oriented toward man's supreme good and is therefore inherently choiceworthy in itself and is a source of genuine human happiness. With the loss of the sense of God as man's supreme good, however, the moral law no longer appears to be the path of life but merely a set of arbitrary rules imposed from without. Thus the obligation to respect the rights of others comes to be seen as a "heteronomy" and contrary to one's own well being. "It is," the pope contends, "the Law as a whole," understood as "good for man in himself," that "fully protects human life." "Detached from this wider framework," the prohibition on killing "is destined to become nothing more than an obligation imposed from without, and very soon we begin to look for its limits and try to find mitigating factors and exceptions."[55] Or, as it is stated more simply in *Veritatis Splendor*: "Those who live 'by the flesh' experience God's law as a burden, and indeed as a denial or at least a restriction of their own freedom."[56] Such men cannot see the good to be gained *for themselves* in preserving the lives of the unborn and the suffering.

This reference to living "by the flesh" points to another consequence of the rejection of love that leads to the culture of death: hedonism. According to John Paul II, the "eclipse of the sense of God and man inevitably leads to a practical materialism, which breeds individualism, utilitarianism and hedonism." Under these conditions, the "only goal which counts is the pursuit of one's own material well-being," and the "so-called 'quality of life' is interpreted primarily or exclusively as economic efficiency, inordinate consumerism, physical beauty and pleasure, to the neglect of more profound dimensions—interpersonal, spiritual and religious—of existence."[57] That is, once man turns from the supreme good, and the genuine happiness, to be achieved through moral virtue and the gift of self, what remains as obviously good, and what comes to dominate his vision of the good, is material comfort or physical pleasure. But once pleasure is taken to be the highest good—or the only, or at least the only publicly acknowledged, good—we must come to find intolerable those lives that are unpleasant, whether our own or those of others. If pleasure is the good, then unpleasant lives cannot be good lives. Such lives seem not only unworthy of protection but in fact to call out for destruction.

If we, rejecting the gospel of life, believe that life is good to the extent that it is pleasant, we are led to endorse the efforts of those who seek to end their lives because they are no longer pleasant and hold out no prospect of future pleasure. Thus we approve of suicide and assisted suicide. To the extent that we take the equation of pleasure and goodness as the closest thing to an objective truth—that is, to the extent that we reject the possibility that genuine happiness might be found in the gift of self, and therefore take pleasure and pain as the only solid realities—we become suspicious of those who choose interminable suffering which death could end. We doubt their grasp of reality, their competence to decide for themselves what course to take. Thus we approve "compassionate" but involuntary euthanasia for the "good" of those who suffer. Finally, to the extent that we are convinced that pleasure is what makes life good, we seek the destruction of those lives that make our own lives less pleasant, those that call for our generosity and self-giving. We come to regard as enemies those whose absolute neediness—the unwanted unborn and the dying—demands our money, our time, and compassion, in sum, our gift of self. Thus we ultimately embrace killing out of cold self-interest.

Evangelium Vitae bears witness to all these connections between hedonism and the culture of death. With regard to hedonism's inclination to suicide and euthanasia, the pope writes that in a pleasure-seeking and materialistic culture "suffering . . . is 'censored,' rejected as useless, indeed opposed as an evil, always and in every way to be avoided. When it cannot be avoided and the prospect of some future well-being vanishes, then life appears to have lost all meaning and the temptation grows in man to claim the right to suppress it." Similarly, he later contends that "[w]hen the prevailing tendency is to value life only to the extent that it brings pleasure and well-being, suffering seems like an unbearable setback, something from which one must be freed at all costs. Death . . . becomes a 'rightful liberation' once life is held to be no longer meaningful because it is filled up with pain and inexorably doomed to even greater suffering." With regard to the connection between hedonism and self-interested homicide, the pope suggests that because of our culture's concern with efficiency "a life which would require greater acceptance, love and care is considered useless, or held to be an intolerable burden, and is therefore rejected in one way or another." Thus one whose existence "compromises the well-being or lifestyle of those who are more favored tends to be looked upon as an enemy to be resisted or eliminated."[58]

TYRANNY AND THE CULTURE OF DEATH

Many probably will think that they can live, and even live contentedly, with what John Paul II condemns as the culture of death. After all, in the developed world there is widespread popular support for somewhat liberal policies with regard to abortion. While there is less support for assisted suicide and euthanasia, these practices, or calls for their legitimization, do not provoke the kind of popular outcry that John Paul II would have thought appropriate. Similarly, the broader theoretical and moral presuppositions of this culture are such as to be quite congenial to many people. After all, those presuppositions—the denial, on the one hand, of objective and universal moral truth, of a supreme good to be achieved through moral self-sacrifice, and the affirmation, on the other hand, of a public hedonism or materialism checked only by some decent but minimal justice and humanity—may well seem to be the basis for the kind of individualistic freedom so valued by most modern human beings.

John Paul II, however, suggests that the implications of the culture of death reach far beyond societal approval of abortion and euthanasia. The pope makes use of the Lord's question to Cain in the book of *Genesis*—"What have you done?"—not only in order to elucidate the causes of attacks on human life, but also to bring to light "the consequences which derive from these attacks for the existence of individuals and peoples." These consequences, he suggests, are most grave. The culture of death, he contends, constitutes a threat "not only to the life of individuals but also to that of civilization itself." More specifically, the attacks on human life that are currently being justified "represent a direct threat to the entire culture of human rights," a "threat capable, in the end, of jeopardizing the very meaning of democratic coexistence: rather than societies of 'people living together,' our cities risk becoming societies of people who are rejected, marginalized, uprooted, and oppressed."[59] Put simply, to embrace the culture of death is to invite outright tyranny.

As noted above, the culture of death denies the objective truth of the moral law as rooted in God. The acceptance of such views, however, necessarily places human beings in an essentially lawless posture with regard to each other. The detachment of freedom from universal and objective truth, John Paul II suggests, "leads to a serious distortion of life in society." Once the "promotion of the self is understood in terms of absolute autonomy, people inevitably reach the point of rejecting one another." Each of one's fellows comes to be viewed as "an enemy from whom one has to defend oneself," and society accordingly becomes "a mass of individuals placed side by side, but without any mutual bonds," each member wishing "to assert himself independently of the other" and actually aiming "to make his own interests prevail" over the other's.[60] As this passage indicates, the denial of objective moral truth not only destroys all principled restraints among men, it also invites them to outright antagonism. Again, in the absence of an objective moral good that is desirable for its own sake, the pursuit of which is the path to human happiness, hedonism or materialism remains as the most obvious value. Popular commitment to material pleasure as the highest good, however, is a recipe for social conflict, for there can never be enough goods to satisfy man's unquenchable physical wants. John Paul II suggests as much in *Sollicitudo Rei Socialis*, where he observes that the "blind submission to pure consumerism" leads "in the first place to crass materialism, and at the same time a radical dissatisfaction, because one quickly learns . . . that the more one possesses the more one wants, while deeper aspirations remain unsatisfied."[61] Thus men are led into conflict over the limited goods for which they all have an infinite desire. Hence the pope's use of a passage from James: "What causes wars, and what causes fightings among you? Is it not your passions that are at war in your members? You desire and do not have."[62]

In principle, then, the relativism and hedonism of the culture of death lead to public chaos. In practice, of course, such consequences are not permitted to follow, for in such a case nobody's well-being would be secure. Thus a truce is reached according to which citizens agree to respect each other's rights, not out of a principled respect for the dignity of each person, but out of a fear of the dangers to oneself that will arise in a lawless society. Again, when objective moral truth is rejected, each person "wishes to assert himself independently of the other and in fact intends to make his own interests prevail." Still, the pope continues, "in the face of other people's analogous interests, some kind of compromise must be found, if one wants a society in which the maximum freedom is guaranteed to each individual." Rights that are established on the basis of such a compromise, however, are far from secure. In this process of merely pragmatic construction of justice, John Paul II contends, "any reference to common values and to a truth absolutely binding on everyone is lost, and social life ventures on to the shifting sands of complete relativism. At that point, everything is negotiable, everything is open to bargaining: even the first of the fundamental rights, the right to life." [63]

Of course, in contemporary circumstances, this process of compromise will be worked out in a democratic context. Thus it might be held that the civil law need not be in conformity with any objective moral law, but need only be the product of majority consensus. As John Paul notes, when "an attitude of skepticism" calls into question "even the fundamental principles of the moral law, the democratic system" is "reduced to a mere mechanism for regulating different and opposing interests on a purely empirical"—that is, a completely amoral—"basis." Nevertheless, he continues, some "might think that even this function, in the absence of anything better, should be valued for the sake of peace in society." That is, even under conditions of widespread moral relativism, a process of mutual pragmatic accommodation of interests can lead to a decent state of public tranquility that provides a tolerable security for most citizens. Indeed, some would go so far as to suggest that moral relativism is "an essential condition of democracy, inasmuch as it alone is held to guarantee tolerance, mutual respect among people and acceptance of the decisions of the majority, whereas moral norms considered to be objective and binding are held to lead to authoritarianism and intolerance." As the pope points out, however, while it is "true that history has known cases where crimes have been committed in the name of 'truth,'" it is no less true that "equally grave crimes and radical denials of freedom have also been committed and are still being committed in the name of 'ethical relativism.'" [64] Moral relativism and its accompanying political pragmatism necessarily imply that rights, even fundamental rights, are not absolute and entitled to defense by any legitimate public authority, but that they are merely a contingent product of political negotiation. In such negotiations, however, all parties are almost never on an equal footing. Thus there is no guarantee that the "peace" produced by such a process will ensure the rights or interests of all. In the absence of objective moral standards, there can be no guarantee that the majority in a given society will respect the rights of the weak—indeed, no principled reason for the strong even to seek to respect the interests of the weak. Thus it is not unlikely that the "peace" arising from a merely pragmatic consensus will be simply illusory, a veil thrown over the domination by some of others who are powerless to resist.

The pope, in fact, considers abortion and euthanasia to be manifestations of just such domination. "When a parliamentary or social majority decrees that it is legal, at least under certain conditions, to kill unborn human life," he asks, "is it not really making a 'tyrannical' decision with regard to the weakest and most defenseless of human beings?" When "relativism" is embraced, he contends, "the 'right' ceases to be such because it is no longer firmly founded on the inviolable dignity of the person, but is made subject to the will of the stronger part."[65] As he implies in his *Letter to Families*, however, in the context of democratic life this "stronger part" must necessarily be made up entirely of adults who have the power to influence the political process. Thus the "right to life becomes an exclusive prerogative of adults who even manipulate legislatures in order to carry out their own plans and pursue their own interests."[66] Under these conditions, the "State is no longer the 'common home' where all can live together on the basis of principles of fundamental equality, but is transformed into a tyrant State, which arrogates to itself the right to dispose of the life of the weakest and most defenseless members, from the unborn to the elderly, in the name of a public interest that is really nothing but the interest of one part."[67] The dying can participate in consensus-formation to a very limited extent, and the unborn not at all. Thus it is not surprising that an amoral, or merely interest-based, consensus regarding rights would fail to protect them.

Again, given widespread doubts about the moral status of the unborn and the true interests of those who are terminally ill and in pain, some might find such a situation acceptable. The pope, however, suggests that the legitimization of abortion and euthanasia already marks the beginning of a "process leading to the breakdown of a genuinely human co-existence and the disintegration of the State itself."[68] After all, once rights are understood pragmatically rather than metaphysically, everyone is in danger, despite the democratic consultation of everyone's interests.

As the pope notes, "[e]ven in participatory systems of government, the regulation of interests often occurs to the advantage of the most powerful, since they are the ones most capable of maneuvering not only the levers of power, but also of shaping the formation of consensus. In such a situation, democracy easily becomes an empty word."[69] Similarly, he contends in *Centesimus Annus* that when democracy is not based on "an adequate account of rights" a "crisis" arises that goes beyond the "scandal of abortion": the all-too-frequent examination of social demands not "in accordance with the criteria of justice and morality, but rather on the basis of the electoral or financial power of the groups promoting them" and a consequent inability to "make decisions aimed at the common good."[70]

Once the moral presuppositions of the culture of death are widely embraced, then, the door is open to all manner of abuse of political power. These consequences are summarized in *Veritatis Splendor*:

> In the political sphere, it must be noted that truthfulness in the relations between those governing and those governed, openness in public administration, impartiality in the service of the body politic, respect for the rights of political adversaries, safeguarding the rights of the accused against summary trials and convictions, the just and honest use of public funds, the rejection of equivocal or illicit means in order to gain, preserve or increase power at any cost—all these are principles which are primarily rooted in, and in fact derive their singular urgency from, the transcendent value of the person and the objective moral demands of the functioning of states. When these principles are not observed, the very basis of political coexistence is weakened and the life of society itself is gradually jeopardized, threatened and doomed to decay.[71]

Indeed, John Paul II goes so far as to suggest that the culture of death and totalitarianism have a common intellectual and moral root. According to him, God alone "constitutes the unshakeable foundation and essential condition of morality, and thus of the commandments, particularly those negative commandments which always and in every case prohibit behavior and actions incompatible with the personal dignity of every man." "Totalitarianism," on the other hand arises out of a denial of truth in the objective sense. If there is no transcendent truth, in obedience to which man achieves his full identity, then there is no sure principle for guaranteeing just relations between people. Their self-interest as a class, group or nation would inevitably set them in opposition to one another. If one does not acknowledge transcendent truth, then the force of power takes over, and each person tends to make full use of the means at his disposal in order to impose his own interests or his own opinion, with no regard for the rights of others. . . . Thus, the root of modern totalitarianism is to be found in the denial of the transcendent dignity of the human person who, as the visible image of the invisible God, is therefore by his very nature the subject of rights which no one may violate—no individual, group, class, nation or State. Not even the majority of a social body may violate these rights, by going against the minority, by isolating, oppressing, or exploiting it, or by attempting to annihilate it.[72]

The ultimate consequences of the system of thought the pope calls the culture of death, then, are most dire and reach far beyond the issues of abortion and euthanasia. Rather, they implicate the question whether any principled commitment to justice among human beings can long be preserved. Thus he contends in *Evangelium Vitae* that the recovery of "those essential and innate human and moral values which flow from the very truth of the human being and express and safeguard the dignity of the person" is "urgently necessary," not only for the sake of the unborn and the aged, but also for "the future of society and the development of a sound democracy."[73]

LIBERAL MODERNITY AND THE CULTURE OF DEATH

John Paul II's critique of the culture of death seems directed primarily at the liberal societies of the developed West. This understanding is first suggested by the pope's observation that, paradoxically, the "tragic repudiation" of the right to life, in the form of abortion and euthanasia, is taking place precisely in that "society which makes the affirmation and protection of human rights its primary objective and boast."[74] A number of other passages in the encyclical elucidate this connection, revealing that many of the moral and intellectual presuppositions of the culture of death are in fact characteristic of the contemporary West's understanding of man and the world.

For example, the turn from God as the supreme good, and the consequent detachment of human freedom from absolute moral principles—which, as we have seen, opens the door to exceptions to the prohibition on homicide, and hence to abortion and euthanasia—is characteristic of the West, on the pope's account. Thus he remarks in *Evangelium Vitae* that it is "especially people in the developed countries" who deny or neglect their "fundamental relationship to God," and who therefore think that man "is his own rule and measure" and demand the right to choose with "complete autonomy" how to live their lives.[75]

Again, hedonism and utilitarianism, the emphasis on "having" over "being," are said in *Evangelium Vitae* to be incitements to the destruction of lives that are impeded in their ability to experience bodily pleasure, or whose neediness demands sacrifices of our own comfort. Yet in *Centesimus Annus* John Paul II implies that such attitudes are to be found primarily in the liberal democracies. For example, in the context of an examination of the "problems and threats emerging within the more advanced economies," the pope mentions "consumerism," an inclination to understand a "better" life as one "directed toward 'having' rather than 'being,'" and to want "to have more, not in order to be more but in order to spend life in enjoyment as an end in itself."[76] Thus he elsewhere suggests that the market-based "consumer society," no less than the Marxism to which it is apparently opposed, excludes "spiritual values," "denies an autonomous existence and value to morality, law, culture and religion," and therefore "totally reduces man to the sphere of economics and the satisfaction of material needs."[77] Such an account of man, as we have seen, invites the destruction of life incompatible with physical comfort by rendering unintelligible the higher goods that might be realized despite bodily pain—the genuine human happiness to be attained through principled obedience to the moral law and finally through the gift of self in love. Despite the inadequacies of the Marxist critique of capitalism, John Paul II accordingly concedes, a kind of "alienation"—in the sense of "the loss of the authentic meaning of human life" and a consequent "moral poverty"—is in fact characteristic of "Western societies."[78]

John Paul II's critique of the culture of death, then, is to a significant extent a critique of the modern West. Less obviously, and perhaps more interestingly, it also appears to be a critique of the modern West *in its very foundations*. This is implied in a passage that appears relatively early in *Evangelium Vitae*. In abortion and euthanasia, and in their increasing public respectability, the pope contends,

> a long historical process is reaching a turning-point. The process which once led to discovering the idea of 'human rights'—rights inherent in every person and prior to any Constitution and State legislation—is today marked by a surprising contradiction. Precisely in an age when the inviolable rights of the person are solemnly proclaimed and the value of life is publicly affirmed, the very right to life is being denied or trampled upon, especially at the more significant moments of existence: the moment of birth and the moment of death.[79]

The pope's reference to the discovery of "rights" that are held to be prior to and binding upon government and positive law calls to mind the ground-breaking work of the early modern political philosophers, as well as the philosophic statesmen, who laid the theoretical and practical foundations of the liberal societies of the modern West. The passage also paradoxically suggests, however, a continuity between the culture of death, the denial of the right to life of some, on the one hand, and, on the other, the early modern discovery of rights. Both the discovery and the denial, it seems, are part of the same "historical process." As we have seen, the pope seems to think that human life is insecure in the West because it is improperly understood: detached from its ultimate end in God, it is viewed materialistically and hedonistically, and therefore its inviolability and the motives to its respect are obscured. The passage under consideration here, however, leads us to suspect that both the misunderstanding and the consequent insecurity can be traced not to some corruption of the modern West's founding principles, but to those very principles themselves. It is perhaps in this light that we can understand John Paul II's remark in an earlier encyclical, *Sollicitudo Rei Socialis*, that the liberal West's concept of "the development of individuals and peoples," no less than the Marxist East's, is "imperfect and in need of radical correction"—that is, a correction that goes to the very roots.[80]

In order to judge whether the seeds of the culture of death really are contained in the origins of modernity, we must turn to an examination of the thought of its intellectual founders. We must turn, in the first place, to Hobbes.

Chapter 3

HOBBES AND THE ORIGINS
OF LIBERAL MODERNITY

There are evident similarities between the social and political teaching of John Paul II, as it appears in *Evangelium Vitae*, and the liberal tradition. The liberal tradition emphasizes the rights of individuals, and in particular the right to life, as the basis of political association. Similarly, John Paul II contends that "every human community and the political community itself are founded" on "recognition" of the right to life.[1] These common concerns can also be found in the thought of Thomas Hobbes, usually held to be the intellectual founder of modern liberalism because of his reorientation of politics toward the protection of the rights and interests of the individual. For Hobbes, the protection of human life is the supreme aim of the political community. The commonwealth, he contends, is a kind of artificial man, "intended" for the "protection and defense" of the natural man. Thus for Hobbes, "*Salus Populi* (the people's safety)" is the commonwealth's "*Businesse*."[2] In fact, for Hobbes the right to life is unalienable, at least in the sense that one can never surrender the right to defend oneself, even against the lawful punishments of the sovereign authority.[3]

Despite such similarities, however, there is also clear evidence of fundamental differences between John Paul II and Hobbes. This evidence is visible even in the introductory portions of their respective works. Recall that John Paul II opens *Evangelium Vitae* by suggesting that human life cannot be properly understood or valued without reference to the highest understanding of life, the life of God. That is, as we have seen, for John Paul II the dignity of human life cannot be securely affirmed apart from a recognition of its divine origins and destiny. In contrast, in the "Introduction" to the *Leviathan*, Hobbes suggests a very different view of life, as "but a motion of limbs."[4] Such a remark betrays a materialism that, on John Paul II's account, must erode respect for human life. Indeed, as we will see, the whole tragedy of liberal modernity's inability to provide a principled defense of the right to life is played out with the greatest clarity in the thought of Hobbes.

REASON, WILL, AND THE STATURE OF MAN

As we have seen, John Paul II contends that we can begin to grasp the basis of man's inviolable dignity by considering him as a creature made in the image and likeness of God. That image and likeness, the pope suggests, is manifested in man's possession of uniquely God-like faculties that radically separate him from the other animals. Man has reason, by which he can discern, and free will, by which he can choose, between good and evil.[5] Hobbes, however, denies these qualities thought by John Paul II to be essential to our respect for human dignity.

Hobbes does, to be sure, classify man as a rational animal. He opens the *Leviathan* by speaking of "that Rationall and most excellent worke of Nature, *Man*," and he elsewhere notes that "the names Man and Rationall, are of equall extent, comprehending mutually one another."[6] Nevertheless, the rationality that man possesses, and that distinguishes him from the other animals, consists for Hobbes not in a capacity to discern between good and evil but merely in an ability to calculate about causes and consequences. Reason, as one of the "Faculties of the mind," is for Hobbes "nothing but Reckoning (that is, Adding and Subtracting) of the Consequences of generall names agreed upon, for the marking and signifying of our thoughts." Again, Hobbes holds that man excels "all other Animals in this faculty," that when he has "conceived any thing whatsoever," he can inquire into "the consequences of it, and what effects he" can "do with it."[7]

That man's intelligence does not, for Hobbes, elevate him above the other animals by giving him access to knowledge of good and evil will become more clear later. For the moment it is sufficient to note Hobbes's definition of prudence. On his view, prudence is simply the ability, derived from experience, to predict future events accurately. A sign, he argues, is "the Event Antecedent, of the Consequent; and contrarily, the Consequent of the Antecedent, when the like Consequences have been observed, before." The more often they have been observed, he continues, the "lesse uncertain is the Signe. And therefore he that has most experience in any kind of business, has most Signes, whereby to guesse at the Future time; and consequently is most prudent." Insofar as animals also make such predictions based on their experience, "it is not Prudence that distinguisheth man from beast."[8]

In contrast, John Paul II sees himself as drawing upon an older intellectual tradition according to which prudence does distinguish man from other animals. In his final book, *Memory and Identity*, John Paul II identifies his position with the "Aristotelian-Thomistic tradition" and contends that Aristotle's *Nicomachean Ethics* is "clearly based upon a genuine anthropology" that has been incorporated into Catholic thought.[9] According to the Aristotelian anthropology, human happiness is realized in the activity of the moral virtues, a view that is echoed, though with distinctively Christian variations, in *Evangelium Vitae*. In the *Ethics*, however, Aristotle rejects a Hobbesian understanding of prudence as mere predictive cleverness and instead defines it as a practical knowledge of how to live out the requirements of the virtues in concrete circumstances. Again, in book 1 of the *Politics*, Aristotle, like John Paul II, contends that man is distinguished from other animals not only by an ability to discern the expedient and the inexpedient, but also the good and the evil.[10]

Finally, it is perhaps worth noting that Hobbes appears to view man's rational faculty, such as it is, not as a sign of his glory and dignity, as does John Paul II, but primarily as a problem, a threat to the peace that is the fundamental aim of the political community. In chapter 17 of the *Leviathan*, Hobbes addresses the question why men cannot live peaceably among themselves in the absence of an artificial sovereign when other animals, like bees and ants, are able to do so on the basis of individual instinct. Hobbes brings forward six reasons for this human incapacity, three of which arise from human rationality. Other animals, "having not (as man) the use of reason, do not see, nor think they see any fault, in the administration of their common businesse: whereas amongst men, there are very many, that thinke themselves wiser, and abler to govern the Publique, better than the rest; and these strive to reforme and innovate" and thus bring the community "into Distraction and Civill warre." Also, because animals lack human rationality, they "want that art of words, by which some men can represent to others, that which is Good, in the likeness of Evill; and Evill, in the likenesse of Good; and augment, or diminish the apparent greatnesse of Good and Evill; discontenting men, and troubling their Peace at their Pleasure." Finally, "irrational creatures cannot distinguish between *Injury*, and *Dammage*; and therefore as long as they be at ease, they are not offended with their fellowes: whereas Man is then most troublesome, when he is most at ease: for then it is that he loves to shew his Wisdome, and controule the Actions of them that governe the Common-wealth."[11] While John Paul II frames human reason primarily in terms of its relation to the supreme good—as a means of attaining union with God through the actions of moral virtue—Hobbes frames it primarily in terms of its contribution to the greatest evil—as a means of deception and disruption that threatens to plunge the community into civil war. One cannot escape the conclusion that for Hobbes it would, in some sense, be better for man not to be human. Such a judgment is hardly the basis for a solid respect for human dignity.

Hobbes is even more emphatic in his denial of free will, the second uniquely human faculty thought by John Paul II to be essential to our recognition of human dignity. Hobbes frankly states that talk of free will is, like that of a *"round Quadrangle,"* absurdity or *"Non-sense,"* a bandying of "words without meaning."[12] Elsewhere he includes free will with the Trinity and transubstantiation as examples of the insignificant and mad speech of the schoolmen.[13]

Human beings, to be sure, *do* will things. Such acts of will are not, however, free, but instead are the outcome of a chain of material causation. "[E]very act of man's will," Hobbes contends, "proceedeth from some cause, and that from another cause, in a continuall chaine, (whose first link is in the hand of God as the first of all causes,).″ Therefore, he concludes, such acts of will "proceed from necessity," and "to him that could see the connexion of those causes, the necessity of all . . . voluntary actions, would appear manifest."[14] On Hobbes's view, will is not something distinct from the passions, but is itself reducible to the passions. He argues that deliberation is nothing more than an alteration of various passions, of hopes and fears about what may arise from performing a possible action. Accordingly, he holds that will is nothing more than the final passion prevailing prior to acting. "In Deliberation, the last Appetite, or Aversion, immediately adhaering to the action, or to the omission thereof, is that wee call the Will; the Act, (not the faculty) of *Willing.*" On this argument, willing, though undeniably a human activity, is by no means a distinctively human activity. If the choices of the human will are no more than the results of a chain of necessary causation, it is clear that the same process will determine the actions of other animals. If will can be understood in terms of the passions, then presumably it must be operative in other passionate animals. Hobbes makes this clear in his discussion of deliberation. The "alternate Succession of Appetites, Aversions, Hopes and Fears" characteristic of deliberation, he contends, is found "no lesse in other living Creatures then in Man." Therefore, "Beasts also Deliberate," and "Beasts that have *Deliberation,* must necessarily also have *Will.*"[15]

For Hobbes, then, human liberty is not, as it is for John Paul II, some metaphysical or spiritual faculty by which man can somehow transcend his passions and freely choose, in light of his discernment of the moral good, among various alternative actions.[16] What remains, then, is for Hobbes to define liberty in terms consistent with his account of the will as unfree. "Liberty, or Freedom," Hobbes states, "signifieth (properly) the absence of opposition" or of "externall Impediments of motion." Again, however, liberty so understood is in no way unique to human beings, but can be "applied no lesse to Irrational" and indeed even to "Inanimate creatures" than to rational ones.[17]

In the thought of Hobbes, those capacities—reason and choice— once thought to confer a special status on man are now presented as marking a mere difference in degree, though not in kind, between man and the lower animals. Man is only a more sophisticated beast, and his superior sophistication is not so much a cause of pride as of difficulty and distress. For Hobbes, then, in contrast to John Paul II, there is nothing God-like in man, nothing sacred in our human nature, no lofty dignity to human life before which we are obliged to stand with some measure of respect and even awe. Thus, from the standpoint of John Paul II's account, Hobbes undermines important inducements to respect for human life.

A RELIGIOUS BEING

According to John Paul II's argument in *Evangelium Vitae*, human dignity, and hence respect for human life, are ultimately based on the loftiness of the human vocation. Man is called to union with God, the supreme good, through obedience to the moral law, even to the point of loving self-sacrifice. This path is, despite its challenges, the true good for man. This view implies that man is by his very nature a moral and sociable being: he realizes his good only in relationship to his fellow men.[18] It suggests further, as we have seen, that man is by nature a religious being, directed toward God as his highest and final fulfillment.

Here, again, Hobbes's teaching radically differs from that of the pope, even though certain superficial similarities may at first mask the deeper disagreements. Hobbes affirms that man is by nature a religious being, or at least that the seeds of religion are planted in man's nature. The belief in and fear of the "Power of Spirits Invisible" is present in man even in the state of nature, "before" the creation of "Civill Society," Hobbes affirms.[19] Similarly, he elsewhere indicates that the "seeds" or "principles" of religion—"an opinion of a Deity, and of Powers invisible, and supernaturall"—can never be completely "abolished out of humane nature."[20] Moreover, for Hobbes, as for John Paul II, man's religiosity makes him unique among the animals. As "there are no signs, nor fruit of Religion, but in Man onely," Hobbes writes, "there is no cause to doubt, but that the seed of Religion, is also onely in Man; and consisteth in some peculiar quality, or at least some eminent degree thereof, not to be found in other Living creatures."[21]

Nevertheless, Hobbes understands man's natural religiosity very differently than does the pope. For John Paul II, recall, man is naturally religious because he possesses a natural orientation toward and longing for God as his supreme good. Created by God in God's own image, and therefore bearing in himself "an indelible imprint of God, man is naturally drawn to God." Again, as Augustine observes, human beings are made for God, and their "hearts are restless until they rest in" him.[22] No doubt on John Paul II's view this happy "rest" reaches its perfection only in the next life; but, as we have seen, he also believes some version of it is possible in this one, through our efforts to unite ourselves to God through the gift of self.

This is far from Hobbes's understanding of the natural root of human religion. Indeed, for Hobbes there is in this life no supreme good in which man's heart can come to rest, and man's heart is therefore doomed to constant restlessness. The "Felicity of this life," Hobbes contends, "consisteth not in the repose of a mind satisfied," for "there is no such *Finis ultimus*, (utmost ayme,) nor *Summum Bonum*, (greatest Good,) as is spoken of in the Books of the old Morall Philosophers." Rather, "Felicity is a continuall progress of the desire, from one object to another; the attaining of the former, being still but the way to the later." Moreover, because man seeks not to enjoy one time alone, but to "assure forever, the way of his future desire," Hobbes posits as "a generall inclination of all mankind, a perpetuall and restlesse desire of Power after power, that ceaseth only in Death."[23]

What, then, is the natural basis of religion, according to Hobbes? The *Leviathan* lays most emphasis upon fear as the root of religious belief. Man's restless quest for power to satisfy his desires, Hobbes suggests, is naturally accompanied by a ceaseless anxiety for the future. It is, Hobbes contends, "impossible for a man, who continually endeavoureth to secure himself against all the evils he feares, and procure the good he desireth, not to be in a perpetuall solicitude of the time to come." Man is inclined, therefore, to have "his heart all the day long, gnawed on by feare of death, poverty, or other calamity," from which he has no repose but in sleep. Moreover, this "perpetuall feare, always accompanying mankind in the ignorance of causes," must have something for its "object." Accordingly, "when there is nothing to be seen, there is nothing to accuse, either of their good, or evil fortune, but some *Power*, or *Agent Invisible*." Thus "the Gods were at first created by humane Feare."[24] For Hobbes, then, in stark contrast to John Paul II, religion arises not from the heart's desire for a transcendent good, but from its affliction by the fear of worldly evils.

To be sure, Hobbes refers to another source of religion, one perhaps less alien to John Paul II's account. While fear of worldly evils is surely the source of belief in the pagan gods, Hobbes argues, "the acknowledging of one God Eternall, Infinite, and Omnipotent, may more easily be derived, from the desire men have to know the causes of naturall bodies, and their severall virtues, and operations; than from the feare of what was to befall them in time to come." For anyone who seeks the cause of effects he observes, and from there seeks the "cause of that cause," and thence plunges "himselfe profoundly into the pursuit of causes, must at last come to this, that there must be (as even the Heathen Philosophers confessed) one First Mover; that is, a First, and an Eternall cause of all things; which is what men mean by the name of God." Moreover, Hobbes emphasizes that the belief in this "God" is not simply a manifestation of man's natural self-interested worldliness, for men come to this belief in a first cause "without thought of their fortune," solicitude for which "gives occasion of feigning of as many Gods, as there be men that feign them."[25] Even here, however, Hobbes's understanding of human religion is quite different from that of John Paul II. Man is directed to this God as first cause by curiosity, not love; and indeed there is nothing in the *Leviathan* to suggest that this first cause merits our love, that it is the same as the God of biblical revelation, whose transcendent goodness demands our love.

AN ASOCIAL AND AMORAL BEING

John Paul II's account in *Evangelium Vitae* suggests that man is by nature a sociable animal. This is implicit in his argument that human beings find their true fulfillment in adherence to the moral law and ultimately in the gift of self; for the moral law lays upon us obligations to our fellow human beings, and the gift of self is given, though ultimately to God, yet most immediately to other persons.

In stark contrast to this view stands Hobbes's argument in the *Leviathan*, and especially the teaching of chapter 13, "Of the Naturall Condition of Mankind, as concerning their Felicity, and Misery." Here Hobbes offers his celebrated account of man's natural asociality, or perhaps even his natural antisociability. It is strange but true, Hobbes contends, that "Nature" tends to "dissociate" men and render them "apt to invade, and destroy one another." This is the necessary consequence of man's natural passions. Men desire the goods that are necessary to their preservation and pleasure, but, given the scarcity of such goods, they are led to fight over them. Such conflict makes men fearful for their lives, and so they are further led to attack each other by way of "Anticipation" or preemption, protecting themselves by destroying their enemies before their enemies can destroy them. Finally, men desire to be honored or valued by other men, and so they attack each other to punish contemptuous treatment. Thus, Hobbes sums up, "in the nature of man, we find three principall causes of quarrell. First, Competition; Secondly, Diffidence; Thirdly, Glory. The first, maketh men invade for Gain; the second, for Safety; and the third, for Reputation."[26]

In addition, Hobbes posits a natural equality of abilities that also contributes to human asociality. While not denying the obvious natural variations in strength of body and mind, Hobbes nonetheless holds that all human beings are equal in the practically decisive respect: "the weakest has strength enough to kill the strongest, either by secret machination, or by confederacy with others, that are in the same danger with himself."[27] Because of this natural equality, the conflict and danger of man's naturally asocial state is naturally unremitting. That is, there can be no expectation that this conflict will be ended by the natural emergence of some winner who will impose his rule and thus bring peace.

Furthermore, as man is naturally asocial, so is he naturally amoral. Because the natural human state is a war of every man against every man, each man has by nature, according to Hobbes, the right to do whatever he thinks expedient in defending himself and his interests. And because "there is nothing he can make use of, that may not be a help unto him, in preserving his life against his enemyes; it followeth, that in such a condition, every man has a Right to every thing; even to one anothers body."[28] If everyone has a right to everything, of course, then no one has a right to anything. That is, everyone has a right to try to get what he needs to survive, but no one has a right to anything that anyone else must respect. Hobbes makes this clear in his denial that there is property in the state of nature. "It is consequent also to the same condition that there be no Propriety, no *Mine* and *Thine* distinct; but only that to be every mans, that he can get; and for so long, as he can keep it." More generally, for Hobbes there is in the state of nature no distinction between justice and injustice. "To this warre of every man against every man, this also is consequent; that nothing can be Unjust. The notions of Right and Wrong, Justice and Injustice there have no place. Where there is no common power, there is no Law; where no Law, no Injustice. Force, and fraud, are in warre the two Cardinall vertues."[29] In sum, for Hobbes all is fair in war; but since war is man's natural state, nothing is wrong by nature.

This is not to say that for Hobbes justice has no existence, but that it has no existence *by nature*. Justice can come into being among men through human artifice, through the erection of a common power capable of making and enforcing law. Such a power comes into being, Hobbes argues, by covenant, an agreement among men to lay down their right to everything and to observe, for the sake of their own preservation, the laws established by the commonwealth. Again, however, this means that in the absence of covenant, and of the law that it makes possible, there is no justice or injustice. Where "no Covenant hath preceded, there hath no Right been transferred, and every man has right to every thing; and consequently, no action can be unjust."[30] Moreover, Hobbes contends, because there can be no valid covenant where there is fear of nonperformance on either side—since men enter into covenants, as they do all things, for the sake of their own well-being—there can be no justice until such fear is removed. That is, there can be no distinction between justice and injustice prior to the establishment of government. Before "the names of Just, and Unjust can have place, there must be some coercive Power, to compell men equally to the performance of their Covenants, by the terrour of some punishment, greater than the benefit they expect by the breach of their Covenant . . . and such power there is none before the erection of a Common-wealth." It is in this spirit that Hobbes defends himself against the charge that he seems to "accuse" human nature in his account of the state of nature. On his own terms, Hobbes cannot be understood as passing a negative moral judgment on man's natural behavior, since by nature alone there are no standards of morality. Hobbes does not accuse man's nature, he says, because the passions of men are no sin, nor "are the Actions, that proceed from those Passions, till they know a Law that forbids them: which till Lawes be made they cannot know: nor can any Law be made, till they have agreed upon the Person that shall make it."[31]

One might object that justice and injustice exist even in the absence of covenant, commonwealth, and law, because the human mind is by nature capable of discerning the difference between good and evil. Again, this would be the view of John Paul II, who holds, as we have seen, that reason's capacity to know the moral law is a faculty men possess by virtue of being created in the image and likeness of God. This view Hobbes denies. His denial—implied in his aforementioned discussion of reason—is made explicit elsewhere in the *Leviathan*. "Justice, and Injustice are none of the Faculties neither of the Body, nor the Mind," Hobbes contends, in a clear rejection of the traditional Christian understanding of conscience.[32] Distinctions between good and evil are not grasped by reason but are simply projections of the human passions. Thus Hobbes holds that whatever a man desires he calls "Good," whatever he hates he calls "evil," and whatever he contemns he calls *"Vile and Inconsiderable."* Such words as these—good, evil, contemptible—are, Hobbes informs us, "ever used with relation to the person that useth them: There being nothing simply and absolutely so; nor any common Rule of Good and Evill, to be taken from the nature of the objects themselves; but from the Person of the man." Because of the absence of some common rule, or because of the radical subjectivity of notions of morality, Hobbes concludes that moral reasoning, understood as an enterprise whereby human beings come to grasp objective moral truths, is impossible. Because different men are pleased and displeased by different things, he argues, the "names of such things as affect us," including the names of the "Vertues, and Vices," are of "inconstant signification" and therefore "can never be true grounds of any ratiocination." Indeed, Hobbes goes so far as to suggest not only that reasoning cannot attain to a moral truth commonly recognized among men, but even that it cannot discern any solid moral truth for any individual. For the passions that give rise to conceptions of good and evil vary not only among men, but also within each man. Because the "constitution" of the human body "is in continuall mutation; it is impossible that all the same things should alwayes cause in him the same Appetites, and Aversions." This, too, is presented by Hobbes as a cause of the "inconstant signification" of names that makes moral reasoning impossible.[33] For Hobbes, then, by nature "private Appetite is the measure of Good, and Evill," and this would seem to be a consequences of his more general understanding of human nature: "the Thoughts, are to the Desires, as Scouts, and Spies, to range abroad, and find the way to the things Desired."[34]

HOBBESIAN HEDONISM

Hobbesian man is not, in contrast to man as understood by John Paul II, a sociable, moral, or religious being. For Hobbes man is not by nature directed to goods beyond himself, such as his fellow men, moral virtue, or God. What remains, then, is that man is directed toward himself. Hobbesian man is fundamentally self-interested. According to Hobbes, "every man by nature seeketh his own benefit, and promotion," and "the proper object of every mans Will, is some Good to himself."[35] More specifically, Hobbesian man is driven primarily by hedonism or material self-interest. Recall that in Hobbes's account of the state of nature, competition for desired goods and fear of losing them are two of the three principal causes of war. Elsewhere, Hobbes remarks that "the greatest part of Mankind" is made up of "[t]hey whom necessity, or covetousnesse keepeth attent on their trades, and labour; and they, on the other side, whom superfluity, or sloth carrieth after their sensuall pleasures."[36]

Hobbes's emphasis on material self-interest represents not only his empirical judgment, however, but also his moral preference. For Hobbes is cognizant of another element in human nature, one that, while still self-interested, nonetheless allows man to transcend a concern with his material well-being. This element is the third cause of quarrel in man's nature, "glory" or pride, which leads men to fight over the "value" that they set upon one another. To frame the issue in terms of the *Republic*'s account of the human soul, Hobbes emphasizes the desiring element, which is concerned with bodily satisfactions, but he is aware of the spirited element, which loves honor and victory. Hence he remarks elsewhere in the *Leviathan* that "the greatest part of Mankind" is made up of not only of "the pursuers of Wealth" and "sensuall Pleasure," but also of "Command."[37] As Plato's Socrates observes, however, and as Hobbes knew well, the spirited part of the soul often leads a man to fight with no regard whatsoever for the bodily pain or damage that he might suffer. It is precisely this spirited indifference to material well-being that Hobbes finds so problematic, however, because it is a threat to the peace that his political teaching aims to secure, and which can be secured on the basis of such materialistic passions as "Feare of Death; Desire of such things as are necessary to commodious living; and a Hope by their Industry to obtain them." Hobbes, then, casts his lot with the hedonistic desires, erecting his commonwealth in their defense, and doing what he can to discredit spiritedness—as, for example, when he dismisses its concerns as "trifles."[38]

Despite his insistence on man's natural self-interestedness and asociality, Hobbes is a moralist, and even a natural law thinker, of a kind. He identifies and defends certain moral principles, and he presents them as somehow grounded in the "Immutable and Eternall" order of nature. Indeed, many of the specific "laws of nature" that Hobbes emphasizes would no doubt be broadly compatible with man's moral nature as understood by John Paul II. Thus among the Hobbesian laws of nature we find such virtues as "gratitude," "compleasance" or trying to accommodate oneself to the needs of others, "pardon," and respect for the equality of one's fellow human beings. Moreover, Hobbes condemns such vices as "pride" and "arrogance." He even formulates his general statement of the law of nature in terms reminiscent of the Bible. Noting that his account of the nineteen laws of nature may involve deductions too subtle for most men to understand, Hobbes says that "to leave all men unexcusable," these laws "have been contracted into one easie sum, intelligible, even to the meanest capacity; and that is, *Do not that to another, which thou wouldst not have done to thy selfe.*"[39]

As we saw earlier, Hobbes's agreement with John Paul II that man is by nature a religious being turns out to be more apparent than real, since they disagree profoundly on what religion is and from what regions of human nature it emerges. The same is true with regard to Hobbes's account of natural law. While Hobbes frames his moral and political teaching in the terms of the natural law tradition on which John Paul II also draws, it is evident that for Hobbes morality is good only in a sense that is very different from that of the pope. Put simply, while for John

Paul II morality is rooted in man's transcendent good, for Hobbes—who, as we have seen, denies the existence of such a good—morality arises from, and is good to the extent that it serves, individual material self-interest.

Hobbes's intention becomes clear when one considers the introduction to his account of the laws of nature. Natural standards of right, he claims, and therefore all natural obligations, derive from man's interest in his self-preservation. "The Right of Nature," Hobbes contends, "is the Liberty each man hath, to use his own power, as he will himselfe, for the preservation of his own Nature; that is to say, of his own Life; and consequently, of doing any thing, which in his own Judgement, and Reason, hee shall conceive to be the aptest means thereunto." Accordingly, a "Law of Nature" is a "Precept, or generall Rule, found out by Reason, by which a man is forbidden to do, that, which is destructive of his life, or taketh away the means of preserving the same; and to omit, that, by which he thinketh it may be best preserved."[40]

While the root of all moral obligation is to be found in individual self-interest, Hobbes is, as a political thinker, concerned with developing a natural law for "Civill Society," one that looks to the establishment of "Peace" among men, "for a means of the conservation of men in multitudes."[41] Yet one should make no mistake about this: for Hobbes the establishment of natural law and the commonwealth is not—and indeed cannot be conceived as—a public-spirited enterprise. Hobbes's teaching seeks that law by which men can be preserved in multitudes, but on his account of human nature individual men are induced to consent to morality, and to the political authority that gives it force, by an interest in *their own* individual self-preservation, not an interest in the preservation of their fellow beings generally. Thus Hobbes is careful to state—in the singular—that "the security of a mans person, in his life, and in the means of so preserving life, as not to be weary of it" is the sole "motive, and end for which" the "transferring of Right" to the sovereign "is introduced."[42] It is in this light that Hobbes understands the aforementioned inalienability of the right to defend one's life, even against the commands of the commonwealth, and even contrary to the interests of the commonwealth and one's fellow subjects. "[N]o man in the Institution of Soveraign Power can be supposed to give away the Right of preserving his own body," Hobbes contends," because, as far as each individual is concerned, it was precisely for the "safety" of that individual body that "all Soveraignty was ordained."[43]

For Hobbes, then, in contrast to John Paul II, adherence to the moral law is only instrumentally, and not intrinsically, good. For the pope, as for the Aristotelian tradition upon which he draws, the actions of moral virtue give expression to man's nature and therefore are a source of his highest happiness. Hobbes repudiates this understanding, however, criticizing the past "Writers of Morall Philosophie" for failing to see "wherein consisted" the "Goodnesse" of the "Vertues," which in fact "come to be praised, as the meanes of peaceable, sociable, and comfortable living."[44] John Paul II also suggests that the moral law is a path of eternal life or union with God as the supreme good, a way of achieving in this life a foretaste of the perfect happiness of the life to come. Again, Hobbes is aware of, and consciously rejects, such a view, noting his disagreement with those who "will not have the Law of Nature, to be those Rules which conduce to the preservation of mans life on earth; but to the attaining of an eternal felicity after death."[45] To revert once more to the language of Plato's *Republic*, John Paul II, like Socrates, understands justice to be among the things desirable both for itself and for its consequences, while Hobbes, with the "many" as described by Glaucon, thinks it good only for its consequences.

This popular, instrumental view of justice set out by Glaucon in the *Republic* reduces justice to a form of "drudgery," a laborious exercise that, though necessary, is inconsistent with man's nature, which instead finds its true joy in "getting the better" of others in the competition for gain.[46] Again, Hobbes does not flinch from acknowledging this consequence, at least implicitly. The state of war, he contends, is "necessarily consequent" to the "naturall Passions of men, when there is no visible Power to keep them in awe, and tye them by feare of punishment to the performance of their Covenants, and observation" of the laws of nature. For "the Lawes of Nature (as Justice, Equity, Modesty, Mercy, and (in summe) doing to others, as wee would be done to,) of themselves, without the terrour of some Power, to cause them to be observed, are contrary to our naturall Passions, that carry us to Partiality, Pride, Revenge, and the like."[47] So for Hobbes the moral law is, in an important sense, contrary to human nature. To revert to the language of John Paul II in *Veritatis Splendor*, the Hobbesian account makes the moral law a kind of "heteronomy," a set of rules extrinsic to man's being. On this view, the goodness of adhering to the moral law becomes a matter of self-interested calculation. Thus Hobbes affirms that we are always obliged to wish that the laws of nature should be obeyed, but are not always obliged in fact to put them into effect: "For he that should be modest, and tractable, and performe all he promises, in such time, and place, where no man els should do so, should but make himselfe a prey to others, and procure his own certain ruine, contrary to the ground of all Lawes of Nature, which tend to Natures preservation."[48]

Hobbes, then, shares the understanding of the origin and nature of justice that is put forward by Glaucon in book 2 of the *Republic*. For both, justice is not rooted directly in man's nature and sought for its own sake, but is an artifice created to protect the weak from the material damage inflicted on them through the injustice of others. Hobbes, however, rejects as an "Errour" the conclusion that Glaucon draws: that for the strong man justice is to be avoided as profitless.[49] Again, Hobbes is earnest about justice. Nevertheless, his earnestness arises not from a principled sense that it is good—morally and spiritually—for the strong to be just, but from the belief that no man is strong enough to profit reliably from injustice. That is, Hobbesian man's commitment to justice is still based on self-interested calculation.

This becomes clear if we consider Hobbes's implicit engagement with, and rejection of, Machiavelli. In chapter 15 of the *Leviathan*, Hobbes considers the view that observance of justice is contrary to reason. Because "every mans conservation, and contentment" is "commited to his own care," it would seem that there "could be no reason, why every man might not do what he thought conduced thereto." Therefore "to make, or not make; keep, or not keep Covenants" seems not to be against reason, when "it conduce[s] to ones benefit." Indeed, injustice would appear sometimes to "stand with that Reason, which dictateth to every man his own good; and particularly then, when it conduceth to such a benefit, as shall put a man in a condition, to neglect not onely the dispraise, and revilings, but also the power of other men." Hobbes concludes that from "such reasoning as this, Successful wickednesse hath obtained the name of Vertue: and some that in all other things have disallowed the violation of Faith; yet have allowed it, when it is for the getting of a Kingdome."[50] One cannot read this passage without calling to mind the serpentine wisdom of *The Prince*.[51]

As we have seen, Hobbes accepts the premise informing this Machiavellian line of reasoning: that human beings are fundamentally self-interested, or that "all the voluntary actions of men tend to the benefit of themselves" and accordingly that "those actions are most Reasonable, that conduce most to their ends." He concludes, however, that this "specious reasoning is neverthelesse false," advancing the following arguments in defense of his break with Machiavelli. First, he notes, we do not say a man has acted reasonably or wisely when he does something that, according to all foreseeable circumstances, "tendeth to his own destruction," yet by some chance happens to turn out to his "benefit." Second, he contends that in the state of war of all against all, "no one can hope to preserve himself by his own strength or wit, but by confederacy with others, where everyone expects the same defense by the Confederation." He that seeks to deceive those who help him will either be cast out of their society and thus perish; or, if he is able to remain in their society, it is only by the errors of the other members, "which he could not foresee, nor reckon upon," and which are "consequently against the reason of his preservation." Finally, he considers the case of the man who gains the sovereignty through rebellion. Here he contends that even when a man succeeds in such an undertaking, "it is manifest" that such success "cannot reasonably be expected, but rather the contrary; and because by gaining it so, others are taught to gain the same in like manner, the attempt thereof is against reason." He concludes, then, that justice or keeping of covenant "is a Rule of Reason, by which we are forbidden to do any thing destructive of our life; and consequently a Law of Nature."[52] In each case, injustice is rejected as unreasonable not because it is contrary to man's nature and therefore productive of unhappiness, but because it is in most foreseeable circumstances an invitation to material damage to the person who undertakes it. That is, Hobbes has no moral disagreement with Machiavelli or with the view of the many as sketched by Glaucon. His disagreement with them is purely practical. While they believe some men are clever and daring enough reasonably to expect to profit from injustice, Hobbes does not. Again, then, for Hobbes observance of the moral law is a matter of calculation about one's material self-interest.

THREATS TO LIFE

As the argument above indicates, Hobbes's political philosophy contains all of the propositions that John Paul II associates with the theoretical underpinnings of the "culture of death." Hobbes and the "culture of death" alike reject God as the supreme good for man and consequently deny the objective truth and intrinsic goodness of the moral law. Both embrace hedonism, viewing physical existence and comfort as man's basic good, and accordingly treat morality as merely instrumental. On John Paul II's account, then, one would expect the Hobbesian teaching to open the door to practical threats to human life. Again, as the pope argues, to the extent that we reject objective moral norms, there is no firm basis on which to erect an absolute prohibition on the destruction of innocent life. And to the extent that we embrace hedonism in preference to the inherent goodness of moral activity, we will be tempted to evade the demands of the moral law when we think such evasion will serve our interests. Thus, on John Paul II's argument, Hobbes's teaching tends in the direction of a legitimization of abortion, suicide, and euthanasia. Such issues are obviously beyond the range of Hobbes's immediate interests, and so they make no explicit appearance in the argument of the *Leviathan*. Nevertheless, one can make a powerful case, on the basis of the text itself, that such consequences indeed follow from Hobbes's teaching.

Let us begin with the question of suicide, because it presents such a clear paradox. Hobbes is celebrated as the philosopher of self-preservation, which, as we have seen, enjoys pride of place as the central concern around which he elaborates his entire teaching. He accordingly contends that one may never surrender the right to defend one's own life. How, then, can his political philosophy incline toward approval of suicide?

Hobbes, to be sure, appears to state, in a passage of capital importance, an absolute obligation to preserve oneself. A "Law of Nature," he says, "is a Precept, or generall Rule, found out by Reason, by which a man is fobidden to do, that, which is destructive of his life, or taketh away the means of preserving the same; and to omit, that, by which he thinketh it may be best preserved."[53] We must also consider another passage, however, one no less crucial to understanding Hobbes's thought: "the Thoughts, are to the Desires, as Scouts, and Spies, to range abroad, and find the way to the things Desired."[54] For Hobbes, reason is subordinate to passion, and reasonable behavior is that which is calculated to fulfill one's desires. We know from common experience, however, from the very fact of suicide, that it is possible for some men to desire death and successfully to seek it out. On Hobbes's own principles, such actions must be, at least for such men, considered reasonable.

If suicide can be reasonable for Hobbes, can it be good? Again, Hobbes's own fundamental principles lead us to this conclusion. Recall that for Hobbes notions of "good" and "evil" are relative to different men according to their divergent passions. Hobbes also admits, however, that some men have extraordinary passions, and even that men can become "weary" of their own lives.[55] Hobbes's teaching thus implies that self-destruction is a "good" action for the man who desires it sufficiently. Hobbes can speak generally of an obligation to preserve oneself because such an obligation conforms to the passions of the general run of men. Nevertheless, when one considers the whole of humanity in light of Hobbes's principles, one is forbidden to conclude that suicide is evil by nature. Of course, the sovereign, taking his moral bearings from the ordinary passions of most human beings, may well forbid suicide. This he has every right to do, as the entire purpose of erecting the sovereignty is to overcome the natural relativism of good and evil and establish an objective rule backed by effective sanctions. For Hobbesian man, however, fear of death is the ultimate inducement to obey the laws decreed by the sovereign. Thus the person with suicidal inclinations is effectively beyond the reach of the standards of right arising from the sovereign's will.

In the case of abortion, we may begin by noting that Hobbes's account of the origins of the social contract includes no place for the unborn. In chapter 13 of the *Leviathan*, Hobbes makes the case that the social contract, the establishment of morality and political authority, arises from the natural insecurity of human beings. This insecurity in turn stems from fundamental human equality: the equality of desires that leads us to compete to get the same scarce things, and the equality of power that allows the weakest to kill the strongest, "either by secret machination, or by confederacy with others, that are in the same danger with himself."[56] This fundamental equality of human beings does not, however, issue in a fundamental equality in the right to life that would include the claims of the unborn. After all, in Hobbes's thought the human right to life is not, as it is for John Paul II, a metaphysically based absolute inherent in the nature of the human person himself. Rather, it is the product of a self-interested calculation. We posit a right to life equally held by all because we are all more or less equally afraid of being killed by each other. It is clear, however, that this calculation alone leads to a dismissal of the claims of the unborn. For the strongest imaginable fetus poses absolutely no threat to the weakest imaginable postnatal human being. Put another way, Hobbes's natural law in defense of life has the nature of a truce; but there is no reason to enter into a truce with those who can inflict no harm.

Moreover, Hobbes's account of the rights of the sovereign authority lays the theoretical groundwork for the liberal abortion regimes of the contemporary Western democracies. This account points to the very practices, and uses the very arguments, of which John Paul II is so critical in *Evangelium Vitae*. We often speak of Hobbes as a defender of absolute monarchy. This is true, but it obscures a certain subtlety in his political theory. Hobbes in fact insists on absolute sovereignty, but merely prefers monarchy. That is, he holds that, for a variety of practical reasons, monarchy is the most stable and desirable form of government, while freely admitting that aristocracy and democracy can also be serviceable in certain circumstances. At the same time, however, the minimal requirements of properly constituted government always and everywhere require that the sovereign authority, whatever form it takes or into whatever hands it is placed, must be understood to be absolute and unlimited. This follows, for Hobbes, from both practical and theoretical considerations. Practically, he contends, absolute sovereignty is necessary to the maintenance of peace, since placing limits on the government's power inevitably creates a justification for rebellion among those who claim that those limits have been overstepped. Theoretically, unlimited governmental power follows from Hobbes's account of the origins of the sovereign. By nature there are no standards of good or evil, and every man has a right to every thing, even the lives of his fellow men. To escape the dangers of this condition they create a sovereign who will himself be the source and measure of good and evil, and who must be understood to possess a power unlimited by any principle other than his own will.

What is the relevance of this understanding to the abortion regimes of the contemporary Western democracies? As the preceding argument indicates, the Hobbesian sovereign, who is possessed of absolute power to determine the content of good and evil, may be not an individual but a corporate institution, may in fact be the ruling majority in a democracy. If such a majority decides, in its political capacity, to authorize its members, in their private capacities, to procure and perform abortions, there is absolutely nothing in Hobbes on the basis of which one could object. As we saw in chapter 2, John Paul II finds the culture of death in the argument that abortion cannot be held to be wrong because it has been authorized by the majority through recognized democratic procedures. This is a perfectly Hobbesian argument.

The implications of Hobbes's principles in this area are further revealed in his account of the family. For Hobbes, parents have by nature an unlimited authority over their children. The sovereign instituted by consent, we recall, possesses absolute power. Hobbes, however, adds that "the Rights and Consequences of both Paternall and Despotical Dominion, are the very same with those of a Sovereign by institution." Thus, where there is no commonwealth instituted, the family itself appears as a kind of little commonwealth, "wherein the Father or Master is the Soveraign." That this paternal power extends to the very existence of the child is made clear by Hobbes later, when he contends that children "are to be taught, that originally the Father of every man was also his Soveraign Lord, with power over him of life and death."[57] For Hobbes, then, it is not contrary to nature for a man to kill his own children.

One might claim, in Hobbes's defense, that on his view the state of nature is an "ill condition" and therefore at best an incomplete guide to his understanding of the kind of justice that should obtain in civil society. If by nature men have the authority to destroy their own offspring, perhaps they surrender such authority upon their entrance into the commonwealth. Indeed, the very passage in which Hobbes affirms the original "life and death" power of fathers over children goes on to note that such power was "resigned" when they instituted the commonwealth. Nevertheless, that such a power is not contrary to nature means that the commonwealth can delegate it back to parents if it so chooses. Hobbes makes this explicit: "the Father, and Master being before the Institution of Common-wealth, absolute Soveraigns in their own Families, they lose afterward no more of their Authority, than the Law of the Common-wealth taketh from them."[58] In sum, for John Paul II the state cannot justly authorize parents to destroy their children, while for Hobbes it can.

One might try to establish a Hobbesian natural law prohibition on the killing of one's children by appealing to the natural desire to preserve them. After all, killing of one's own offspring must ordinarily run counter to normal human desires, and Hobbes's teaching seeks to base natural law on the most powerful human passions.[59] Hobbes appears to lend some equivocal support for such a view. Even in the *Leviathan*'s account of the state of nature, Hobbes seems to insert an unobtrusive reservation in favor of some elementary human sociability when he concedes that the government of small families depends on "naturall lust." Might we not read this remark as implying that the community of husband, wife, and children is held together by a kind of natural sympathy that interests each member in the well-being of the others? One's hopes for such a reading of this passage, however, seem to be dashed by the definitions Hobbes has laid down earlier in the work. For "naturall lust," Hobbes informs us, is nothing more than the "Love of Persons for Pleasing the sense onely." Whatever bond the pleasure of the senses might create between man and woman, it is doubtful that Hobbes intends it to refer to an emotional bond between parents and children. On the other hand, Hobbes elsewhere speaks of the state of nature as possessing no laws "but the Law of Nature, and the naturall inclination of the Sexes one to another, and to their children."[60]

The ambiguous status of parental affection in Hobbes's account of the hierarchy of human values is resolved elsewhere in the *Leviathan*, and in a direction that is not beneficial to the interests of children. In his discussion of the "Office of the Soveraign Representative," in chapter 30 of the *Leviathan*, Hobbes speaks of the sovereign's obligation to see that justice is taught to his subjects. He notes that of the "things held in propriety, those that are dearest to a man are his own life, and limbs; and in the next degree, (in most men,) those that concern conjugall affection; and after them riches and means of living." Consequently, the people must be instructed "to abstain from violence to one anothers person, by private revenges; from violation of conjugall honour; and from forcible rapine, and fraudulent surreption of one anothers goods." On Hobbes's view, children are not to be found among the top three things about which men care, and accordingly one's duty to them is not part of the necessary public catechism in the rudiments of justice. Indeed, in this same chapter Hobbes asserts that parental care is the result not of self-giving love but of self-interested calculation. The duty to honor parents must be acknowledged, he says, because there would not be "any reason" for parents to "desire to have children, or take the care to nourish and instruct them, if they were afterwards to have no other benefit from them, than from other men."[61] In the end, then, Hobbes remains scrupulously faithful to the individualistic foundations of his system even in his account of the family.

In light of these passages, it is not surprising that the *Leviathan* reveals its author's capacity to speak of infanticide in measured tones as apparently no matter of great moment one way or the other. By nature, he contends, dominion over a child belongs first to its mother; and this dominion may be exercised either to foster the child or let it die from neglect. The "Infant is first in the power of the Mother, so as she may either nourish, or expose it; if she nourish it, it oweth its life to the Mother; and is therefore obliged to obey her, rather than any other; and by consequence the Dominion over it is hers. But if she expose it, and another find, and nourish it, the Dominion is in him that nourisheth it. For it ought to obey him by whom it is preserved."[62]

None of this is to say, of course, that Hobbes would recognize anything like the "right" to abortion often asserted in contemporary American politics. Such a right depends on constitutional notions of limited government or philosophic notions of self-ownership, notions that Hobbes consistently denies. There can be no sphere of privacy into which government must not enter, because for Hobbes there must be no limits at all on the sovereign's authority. There can be no self-ownership held against the state, because for Hobbes the civil law absolutely determines what everyone may rightly claim to possess. In sum, for Hobbes there is no right to abortion because the sovereign alone may determine what rights subjects possess. This is as much as to say, however, that for Hobbes human beings as such have no rights at all, which notion is an essential element of what John Paul II understands to be the "culture of death."

TYRANNY

The observation that for Hobbes human beings as such have no rights at all recalls for us John Paul II's account of the ultimate consequences of the hedonism and materialism of the culture of death, consequences that cannot be confined to suicide and abortion. For, on the pope's argument, once we subordinate the moral law to individual material well-being, there is nothing to stop *all* human lives from being valued not for their mere humanity but only conditionally, as a result of a utilitarian calculus. Once again, such consequences are drawn out with admirable lucidity by Hobbes: "The Value, or Worth of a man, is as of all things, his Price; that is to say, so much as would be given for the use of his Power: and therefore is not absolute; but a thing dependent on the need and judgement of another." Human beings, Hobbes indicates, have no inherent worth, and their value can be established, like that of any other commodity, by the operation of the market: "And as in other things, so in men, not the seller, but the buyer determines the Price. For let a man (as most men do,) rate themselves at the highest Value they can; yet their true value is no more than it is esteemed by others."[63]

Hobbes's teaching in the *Leviathan* confirms John Paul II's contention that the embrace of such an understanding of human worth must open the door to tyranny. At the most general level, we may first observe that to be rejected, tyranny must first be named. That is, one requires some objective standard of what constitutes "injustice" if one is to condemn any particular government or policy as tyrannical. Hobbes, however, completely dismantles the intellectual structures by which such judgment is possible. For the pope, as for the Aristotelian and Thomistic tradition on which he draws, there are principles of right prior to and, in a sense, above the civil law, natural principles of right in light of which human laws can be rationally evaluated as good or bad. To the extent that civil law deviates from the moral law, to that extent the former is unjust. Hobbes, on the other hand, when he asks "what are good laws," comments that the answer cannot be "just ones, for no law can be unjust." The civil laws cannot be judged by men because those laws are themselves the standard of good and evil, terms that by nature have no objective significance. Hence Hobbes's insistence that tyranny is not really a genuine, rationally discernible form of government, as Aristotle held, but merely "monarchy misliked."[64]

It is in this spirit that Hobbes speaks of governmental actions once thought to be tyrannical—such as the expropriation of a subject's property for the sake of its transfer to a "favourite or flatterer" of the king—not as unjust but as merely inconvenient.[65] The consequences of his teaching are still more grave, however: for Hobbes the sovereign may justly destroy the innocent. Again, such consequences are implied by Hobbes's fundamental principles, and Hobbes does not shrink from explicitly drawing out these implications, with all his accustomed clarity. As we have seen before, Hobbes holds that justice and injustice have no place in the state of nature, where all men have a right to everything, including to each other's bodies or lives. Thus, when a political community is instituted, those who choose not to become members remain "in the condition of warre" in respect to the others and are therefore subject to being "destroyed" by the others "without injustice."[66] Accordingly, the sovereign has the right to advance the interests of the commonwealth by killing those outside of it, whether they are innocent or not. The "Infliction of what evill soever, on an Innocent man, that is not a Subject, if it be for the benefit of the Common-wealth, and without violation of any former Covenant, is no breach of the Law of Nature," Hobbes contends:

> For all men that are not Subjects, are either Enemies, or else they have ceased from being so, by some precedent covenants. But against Enemies, whom the Common-wealth judgeth capable to do them hurt, it is lawfull by the originall Right of Nature to make warre;

wherein the Sword Judgeth not, nor doth the Victor make distinction
of Nocent, and Innocent, as to the time past; nor has other respect of
mercy, than as it conduceth to the good of his own People.[67]

Again we see that for Hobbes human beings as such have no rights and
are not entitled even to some minimal respect for justice in the sovereign's dealings with them. Those outside the commonwealth for which
the sovereign is responsible may be destroyed not for any harm they
have done or intend, but simply for being capable of doing harm.

If the innocent human being as human being has no right to life
that the sovereign must respect, one wonders whether such a right
can be securely possessed by the sovereign's subjects. That is, if being
a member of the human community confers no moral status that the
state must respect, is such status securely conferred by membership in
the particular political community for which the state is responsible?
The fragility of one's status as subject, and therefore the fragility of
whatever justice one is owed as a subject, is revealed in the immediate
sequel to Hobbes's aforementioned account of the sovereign's right to
destroy even innocent nonsubjects. Subjects "who deliberately deny the
Authority of the Common-wealth," he argues, place themselves again in
the state of war, and accordingly are made to "suffer" for their actions
"not as Subjects, but as Enemies." Thus the "vengeance" of the sovereign reaches not only these former subjects themselves, but "is lawfully
extended . . . to the third and fourth generation not yet in being, and
consequently innocent of the fact, for which they are afflicted."[68] For
Hobbes, it seems, one's status as a subject, and hence whatever justice
one is owed as a subject, can be forfeited by the actions of others, at the
judgment of the sovereign.

In truth, however, the Hobbesian sovereign may extinguish the innocent without even bothering to revoke subject status. Even the innocent
subject has no right to life that the sovereign is bound to respect. After
all, for Hobbes justice and injustice have no place in the state of nature.
Human beings escape from the state of nature, and establish justice, by
means of a covenant that creates a sovereign authority. As Hobbes is at
pains to point out, however, the covenant that establishes the sovereign
is *among* those instituting the sovereignty, and not *between* them and the

person on whom they confer the sovereignty.[69] Thus on his view the institution of sovereignty puts an end to the state of nature among subjects, but not between them and the sovereign, who, consequently, remains completely free to dispose of those under his authority at his own discretion. Hobbes thus concludes that no action of the sovereign towards his subjects can be understood as an injustice.[70] Therefore, he argues, "a Subject may be put to death, by the command of the Soveraign Power; and yet neither doe the other wrong: As when *Jeptha* caused his daughter to be sacrificed: In which, and the like cases, he that so dieth, had Liberty to doe the action, for which he is neverthelesse, without injury put to death. And the same holdeth also in a Soveraign Prince, that putteth to death an Innocent Subject." It is worth noting that Hobbes presents this not merely as a theoretical implication of his teaching, but as the sort of thing that "may, and doth often happen in Common-wealths."[71]

HOBBES AND CHRISTIANITY

In light of the argument of this chapter, the thought of Hobbes would seem to embody all the principles and consequences diagnosed in our own day by John Paul II as "the culture of death." One might, however, raise a final objection to this conclusion. Hobbes appears to write as a Christian. Does not his acknowledgment of a God who is above the commonwealth place moral limits on what the sovereign can do to its subjects? Indeed, Hobbes invites this conclusion even in the passage in which he claims that the sovereign can kill the innocent without doing injustice. David's killing of Uriah, though not injustice, nevertheless was "against the law of Nature, as being contrary to Equittie," and hence an injury to God, because David, though king, was nonetheless God's subject. Elsewhere, Hobbes indicates more generally that "there is that in heaven" which the sovereign "should stand in fear of, and whose Lawes he ought to obey."[72]

Nevertheless, Hobbes seems less to be guided by traditional Christianity than interested in transforming it in order to render it compatible with, or at least less incompatible with, his political teaching. He hints at such an intention in the dedication to the *Leviathan*, in which he predicts that his work might "offend" some by its use of "certain Texts of Holy Scripture, alleged by me to other purpose than ordinarily they use to be by others." These modifications are necessary, he claims, because such scriptures are "the Outworks of the Enemy, from whence they impugne the Civill Power."[73] Hobbes's reforms of Christianity are so radical that they lead to suspicions concerning the sincerity of his belief: some scholars accuse Hobbes of concealing unbelief behind a facade of rhetorical piety, and in fact such suspicions were entertained by his contemporaries even during his lifetime.[74]

We cannot attempt here a thorough investigation of Hobbes's treatment of religion. It will be sufficient to our purpose to offer a few observations showing that his invocations of God in the Leviathan place no principled moral restraints on the sovereign. In the religious tradition to which Hobbes is responding, God's law is commonly thought to be known through both revelation and reason. God's revealed law does not effectively bind the sovereign, on Hobbes's view, because the sovereign himself is held to be the mediator of revelation. Christians, Hobbes teaches, should take their Christian sovereign as God's prophet. Unless one is privy to a supernatural revelation communicated directly from God himself, Hobbes contends, one cannot know whether a particular claimed revelation is in fact genuine. Thus one must leave the question to be determined by the political authority. When there is a question as to what "God hath said," for those who have no supernatural revelation themselves the truth of the matter "cannot be known, but by that naturall reason, which guided them, for the obtaining of Peace and Justice, to obey the authority of their severall Common-wealths." Thus the sovereign is authorized to appoint pastors and even determine the canon of scripture.[75]

Hobbes also mentions those "Divine Lawes" that are "Dictates of Naturall Reason" concerning the "naturall Duties of one man to another." These, he says, are the "same Lawes of Nature" as he discusses in chapters 14 and 15 of Leviathan, "namely, Equity, Justice, Mercy, Humility, and the rest of the Morall Vertues." As we have seen, however, Hobbes understands these virtues as being good only conditionally, on the basis of a kind of utilitarian calculation. They are merely the "meanes of peaceable, sociable, and comfortable living."[76] Being of no intrinsic value, sovereigns will feel justified in disregarding them if their society's, or their own, interests can be so advanced.

Still, a God who is a lawgiver may also be a law-enforcer. Might not the Hobbesian sovereign be led to a consistent respect for the laws of nature, and hence for the rights of subjects, by a fear that God will punish violations of His law? Hobbes appears to do what he can to undermine belief in such a providential and righteous God, and hence to render the utilitarian defense of morality the only one operative in his thought. It is true, as we have seen, that he argues for a natural knowledge of God as the first cause. He also adds, however, that men cannot "have any Idea of him in their mind, answerable to his nature."[77] Elsewhere, Hobbes contends that while we may grant God certain attributes with a view to honoring him, we do not in fact know anything about these attributes, so that they are not to be taken as signifying any "Philosophicall Truth." Interestingly, Hobbes includes among God's attributes his "existence," thus indicating that we cannot even know whether God exists, let alone whether he is concerned with upholding the law of nature.[78]

CONCLUSION

It is striking that the whole array of intellectual and moral causes and consequences that John Paul II labels the "culture of death"—the denial of a transcendent good, and of the objective and intrinsic goodness of the moral law, the affirmation of hedonism and utilitarianism, and the consequent vulnerability of human life and openness to tyranny—can be found articulated with perfect clarity in the thought of Hobbes. Yet Hobbes is admitted on all sides to be one of the chief intellectual architects of liberal modernity. His influence can be seen in the work of almost all subsequent modern political thinkers. One is therefore led to wonder whether what the pope terms the "culture of death" is somehow embedded in the philosophic foundations of modernity itself.

Nevertheless, Hobbes is also a very controversial figure, even and especially among his successors, the other philosophic founders of liberal modernity. Hobbes's tremendous influence can be seen not only in the extent to which others have followed his turn to the interests of the individual as the basis of political society, but also in the reaction provoked in those critical of his absolutist conclusions. Moreover, we cannot deny even Hobbes's good intentions. Like those of whom John Paul II is critical in *Evangelium Vitae*, he denied the existence of a transcendent standard of good and evil, and insisted on the absolute sanctity of civil law, because he thought such a teaching necessary to secure peace and order: those who appeal to a higher law are tempted to a violent fanaticism that destroys public peace and consequently every other worldly good. We may not simply say, then, that the "culture of death" is integral to the foundations of liberal modernity, much less that the two are equivalent. We may say, however, that liberal modernity contains the seeds of a powerful temptation in the direction of this "culture of death" and the tyranny to which it gives rise. To see to what extent this temptation has been successfully resisted, we must turn to other, more moderate accounts of liberal modernity. We must turn to John Locke.

Chapter 4

LOCKE'S THEISTIC LIBERALISM

From the standpoint of John Paul II's concerns, the political philosophy of John Locke must appear, at least at first glance, as altogether more sound than that of Hobbes. To begin with, unlike Hobbes, Locke undertakes in his primary and most public political works—the *Two Treatises of Government*—no rejection of free will or express demotion of reason to mere calculation. Locke offers no explicit Hobbesian denial of man's natural sociability, nor of reason's natural ability to discern the difference between good and evil. Indeed, Locke famously differs from Hobbes both in the starting point of his political reasoning and in its conclusion. While Locke, like Hobbes, posits a prepolitical state of nature, he also contends that there is a law of nature that obliges man even in this state. And while the combination of Hobbes's moral relativism with his advocacy of absolute sovereignty makes it easy to charge his system with an openness to tyranny, Locke forthrightly departs from Hobbes in advocating limited government, in naming government that surpasses those limits tyrannical, and in countenancing disobedience and even rebellion as justifiable responses to the radical abuse of public power.

Nevertheless, there are aspects of Locke's thought that appear, on John Paul II's account, problematic. Locke clearly does not simply recapitulate, but instead appears to revise, the Aristotelian and Catholic understanding of human nature and the nature of morality on which John Paul II draws. To the extent that our understanding of these things is, for John Paul II, essential to sustaining a proper respect for the dignity of human life, we may wonder whether he would regard Locke's teaching as providing some opening to the culture of death. We turn to Locke's political teaching with a view to exploring this question.

LOCKE'S THEISTIC NATURAL LAW

Locke differs most obviously from Hobbes, and seems to move in the direction of John Paul II, in that he repeatedly affirms the existence of an objective natural law rooted in the will of God the creator. Locke is, to be sure, a state of nature theorist, and accordingly he begins from presuppositions that are in some respects similar to those of Hobbes. Locke holds that men are by nature in a prepolitical state of perfect freedom and equality. In this state all men may "order their Actions, and dispose of their Possessions, and Persons as they think fit . . . without asking leave, or depending upon the Will of any other Man." Moreover, among men in the state of nature "all the Power and Jurisdiction is reciprocal, no one having more than another."[1]

Nevertheless, Locke departs radically from Hobbes in his understanding of the status of morality in the state of nature. Hobbes, as we have seen, holds that the state of nature is utterly lawless. Terms like justice and injustice, good and evil, have no place there. Such principles can only come into existence with the creation, by agreement, of a sovereign who will make laws defining and enforcing principles of right and wrong. Hobbes does not merely claim that justice cannot be vindicated in the state of nature; rather, it has no existence at all. Hence his argument that human reason is powerless to discern the difference between good and evil, notions of which are merely fleeting manifestations of men's constantly changing passions.

In contrast, Locke insists that the state of nature contains a law of nature that is accessible to human reason and that imposes certain obligations on men to one another, most especially an obligation to preserve human life. Locke's initial description of the state of nature offers a qualification of man's natural freedom not found in Hobbes: men are free to dispose of themselves and their possessions, Locke says, "*within the bounds of the Law of Nature."*[2] Thus the state of nature, while a "State of Liberty," is emphatically not a "State of License" in which men may simply do anything they wish in the absence of any moral restraints. While men in the state of nature possess liberty to dispose of themselves and their property according to their own judgment, this liberty is not absolute: for man in the state of nature "has not Liberty to destroy himself, or so much as any Creature in his Possession, but where some nobler use, than its bare Preservation, calls for it."[3] Locke's classic statement of the law of nature limiting man's natural freedom runs as follows:

> The State of Nature has a Law of Nature to govern it, which obliges every one: And Reason, which is that Law, teaches all Mankind, who will but consult it, that being all equal and independent, no one ought to harm another in his Life, Health, Liberty, or Possessions. For Men being all the Workmanship of one Omnipotent, and infinitely wise Maker; All the Servants of one Sovereign Master, sent into the World by his order and about his business, they are his Property, whose Workmanship they are, made to last during his, not one another's Pleasure. And being furnished with like Faculties, sharing all in one Community of Nature, there cannot be supposed any such Subordination as if we were made for one another's uses, as the inferior ranks of Creatures are for ours. Every one as he is bound to preserve himself, and not to quit his Station willfully; so by the like reason when his own Preservation comes not in competition, ought he, as much as he can, to preserve the rest of mankind, and may not unless it be to do Justice to an Offender, take away, or impair the life, or what tends to the Preservation of the Life, Liberty, Health, Limb or Goods of another.[4]

The contrast with Hobbes could not be more clear. For Locke, apparently, human reason can discern moral principles obliging men to each other, even in the absence of government and law. Hence Locke's clearly non-Hobbesian suggestion that man is moral by his very nature, and not only artificially by the institution of society: "Truth and keeping of Faith belongs to Men, as Men, and not as Members of Society."[5] Indeed, several of Locke's key contentions—for example, that reason can discern the law of nature obliging man to his fellows, that man is by his very nature a moral being, and that life is ultimately God's property and therefore not to be destroyed by man—all have echoes in John Paul II's argument in *Evangelium Vitae*.

It is precisely Locke's insistence on this prepolitical moral law that allows him to avoid what John Paul II would surely regard as the tyrannical conclusions of Hobbes's teaching. The Lockean magistrate, unlike the Hobbesian sovereign, is not the source of good and evil but is himself subject to it. Regardless whether "Princes are exempt from the Laws of their Countrey," Locke writes, "I am sure, they owe subjection to the Laws of God and Nature. No Body, no Power can exempt them from the Obligations of that Eternal Law."[6] These differences between Hobbes and Locke follow from their different understandings of the state of nature and the extent of man's freedom within it. For both thinkers, government is man's artificial creation, yet they differ on the powers of the invention because they differ on the powers of the inventor. For Hobbes, as we have seen, man is absolutely free by nature, with a right to all things, and thus he can—and, on Hobbes's view, should—transfer this unlimited power to the sovereign. For Locke, conversely, even prepolitical man is under a law of nature that limits his power over himself and others and therefore of necessity limits the power that he can assign to the government in whose creation he participates. The legislative power of the commonwealth, though supreme, cannot be "absolutely *Arbitrary* over the Lives and Fortunes of the People," Locke argues. For that power is nothing but "the joynt power of every Member of the Society given up to that Person, or Assembly, which is Legislator," and can therefore "be no more than those persons had in a State of Nature before they enter'd into Society, and gave up to the Community. For no Body can transfer to another more power than he has in himself; and no Body has an absolute Arbitrary Power over himself, or over any other, to destroy his own Life, or take away the Life or Property of another."[7]

Man's natural freedom, his power, is guided by a natural law, a law that intends the preservation of human life. The power man transfers to government is both limited and informed by that same law of nature. The legislative authority of the commonwealth, Locke contends, "is a power that hath no other end but preservation, and therefore can never have a right to destroy, enslave, or designedly to impoverish the Subjects." Locke sums up his teaching as follows:

> [T]he Law of Nature stands as an Eternal Rule to all Men, Legislators as well as others. The Rules that they make for other Mens actions, must, as well as their own and other Mens Actions, be conformable to the Law of Nature, i.e. to the Will of God, of which that is a Declaration, and the *fundamental Law of Nature*, being *the preservation of Mankind*, no Humane Sanction can be good, or valid against it."[8]

Elsewhere Locke does not hesitate to label as tyrannical those actions of government that depart from the law of nature and are destructive of life or of man's other natural rights.[9]

We saw in the previous chapter that Hobbes's teaching anticipates contemporary justifications for some societies' permissive policies with regard to abortion, assisted suicide, and euthanasia, specifically the argument that democratic majorities have the authority to withdraw the protection of the law from certain classes of human life, and even to authorize its destruction. On this Hobbesian view, there must be no appeal to standards of justice beyond those set down by the ruling authority, and thus that authority itself becomes the source of standards of good and evil, even in regard to the most fundamental rights. John Paul II, of course, contends that such policies are in substance tyrannical regardless of their having been enacted through democratic procedures, because he insists on the existence of an objective moral law which not even democratic majorities have the authority to revoke or revise. We may note here that on this broad principle Locke's teaching is in agreement with the pope's. In his discussion of tyranny, Locke contends that it is a "Mistake to think this Fault is proper only to Monarchies," for "other forms of Government" are just as "liable to it." Whenever government power, which is intended for the preservation of the people's rights to life, liberty, and property, is turned to other purposes, "and made use of to impoverish, harass, or subdue them to the Arbitrary and Irregular Commands of those that have it," it "becomes *Tyranny*, whether those that use it thus are one or many."[10]

Hobbes, as we have seen, implicitly teaches that the sovereign could without injustice authorize parents to destroy their own children. Locke, however, denies the foundation of this Hobbesian view: that parents by nature possess a power of life and death over their offspring. Indeed, Locke devotes considerable attention to the paternal power, repeatedly denying that it extends to a right to deprive children of their lives.[11] Moreover, Locke elsewhere expressly links this prohibition to his theistic formulation of the law of nature, which requires that men seek to preserve human life as the handiwork of God. Some, Locke notes, contend that "Fathers have a power over the Lives of their Children, because they give them Life and Being." Locke responds that, aside from the fact that those who give something may not always have a right to take it back, those who advance this argument forget that God "is the Author and Giver of Life."[12]

Locke's emphasis on natural duties of benevolence draws his teaching even closer to that advanced in *Evangelium Vitae*. Recall that for John Paul II the commandment, "You shall not kill," is not to be understood only negatively, as prohibiting the destruction of human life, but also positively, as enjoining an active care for it. Similarly, Locke's law of nature imposes positive obligations on human beings to care for each other. This becomes most clear in his discussion of familial duties. As we have seen, Hobbes discusses the practice of exposure, or of passive infanticide, in matter-of-fact terms, in part because he does not accord parental affection a very prominent place in human nature, and moreover because he accords to parents a naturally unlimited power over their offspring. In contrast, Locke speaks of such practices as a disgrace to human nature. Those who use the practice of sale or exposure of children to show that parents have absolute power over their offspring, Locke argues, base their opinion on "the most shameful Action, and most unnatural Murder, human Nature is capable of." God has given parents "Charge and Care of" their children, and he requires the former to preserve the latter "by the Dictates of Nature and Reason, as well as his Reveal'd Command," which even unintelligent animals ordinarily take care to observe.[13] Thus children have, "by the appointment of God himself, who hath thus ordered the course of nature, a Right to be nourish'd and maintained by their Parents, nay a right not only to a bare Subsistence but to the conveniences and comforts of Life, as far as the conditions of their Parents can afford it."[14] Of course, the parents' obligation to preserve their children is accompanied by a kind of government, a "power of commanding and chastising." Yet, Locke is quick to add, "God hath woven into the Principles of Humane Nature such a tenderness for their Off-spring, that there is little fear that Parents should use their power with too much rigour; the excess is seldom on the severe side, the strong byass of Nature drawing the other way."[15] In sum, while for Hobbes the right to life of children finds scant support in either the laws of nature or the natural human passions, it finds strong support in both for Locke.

Furthermore, for Locke this natural positive obligation to render aid in support of life extends beyond the family and becomes a duty to humanity generally. This is suggested in his foundational statement of the law of nature, which notes that everyone is "bound" not only "to preserve himself, and not to quit his Station willfully," but also "by the like reason" to "preserve the rest of mankind," at least "as much as he can," when "his own Preservation comes not in competition" with that of others. Thus he concludes that one "may not unless it be to do Justice to an Offender, take away, or impair the life, or what tends to the Preservation of the Life, Liberty, Health, Limb or Goods of another."[16] While the latter formulation may imply nothing more than an obligation to refrain from harming others, Locke elsewhere makes clear that his law of nature imposes an affirmative duty to help human beings preserve their lives. We know, he contends in the *First Treatise*, that "God hath not left one Man so to the Mercy of another, that he may starve him if he please." Rather, God has given no man "such a Property, in his peculiar Portion of the things of this World, but that he has given his needy Brother a Right to the Surplusage of his Goods; so that it cannot justly be denied him, when his pressing Wants call for it."[17] Indeed, Locke indicates that this obligation to help applies even between those who have only just emerged from a state of war. In his discussion of conquest, Locke brings to light a likely conflict of claims to the property of the conquered. On the one hand, the conqueror has a right to that property for the sake of reparation, for the sake of making up the losses imposed on him by the now-defeated aggressor. On the other hand, the wife and children of that aggressor are entitled to his property for their own support. Locke solves the dilemma as follows: "The Fundamental Law of Nature being, that all, as much as may be, should be preserved, it follows, that if there be not enough fully to *satisfy* both, *viz.* for the Conqueror's Losses, and Childrens Maintenance, he that hath, and to spare, must remit something of his full Satisfaction, and give way to the pressing and preferable Title of those, who are in danger to perish without it."[18]

As we have seen, according to John Paul II adequate security for human life demands that the moral law be understood as encompassing love, as requiring that we protect and serve life. One could say, in light of the preceding argument, that there appears in Locke's teaching a natural law that looks toward something like John Paul II's understanding, that looks toward love or a duty of generosity to those in need. Moreover, Locke, like John Paul II, presents this moral teaching as rooted in God and accessible to human reason. To this extent, a Lockean modernity might appear far less inclined to what *Evangelium Vitae* terms the culture of death than does a Hobbesian modernity.

LOCKE'S PROBLEMATIC ANTHROPOLOGY

Nevertheless, Locke's teaching presents certain difficulties. For the *First and Second Treatises* contain elements that can only be termed Hobbesian, elements that tend to undermine the decent natural law on which Locke insists so vigorously in the aforementioned passages.[19] Locke tends to place individual self-interest at the center of human nature, and he often adverts to a materialism or hedonism that is reminiscent of Hobbes. His emphasis on comfortable self-preservation tends implicitly to deny, or at least to marginalize, the higher ends of human life. On the argument of *Evangelium Vitae*, however, human life cannot be properly valued unless it is understood in light of its loftiest activities. Thus, from the standpoint of John Paul II, these elements in Locke's thought must tend to warp his understanding of the value of human life and therefore undermine his account's ability fittingly to safeguard it.[20]

Consider Locke's account of human sociability. Again, John Paul II's argument suggests a rather rich understanding of man's natural relatedness to his fellows, especially insofar as the pope holds that man realizes his nature most perfectly through the gift of self to others. In stark contrast, Hobbes, as we have seen, views men as naturally asocial and indeed at war with one another. Locke, without going so far as John

Paul II, still seems to recognize a natural gregariousness in men. Thus he remarks that men incorporate themselves into social bodies not only because of the "inconveniencies" of the state of nature, but also for "the love, and want of Society."[21] Unlike for Hobbes, then, for Locke human sociability is not wholly artificial: men unite not only with a view to advancing their individual material interests but also because they are naturally inclined to enjoy each other's company.

Despite the presence of such remarks, however, the weight of Locke's account inclines in a more Hobbesian direction. Locke appears to embrace Hobbes's belief that man is fundamentally a self-interested being. Therefore, while he acknowledges a law of nature and a natural human sociability, neither is, on Locke's account, sufficient to make the state of nature livable. Locke contends that men are willing to resign the freedom they possess in the state of nature because that state "is full of fears and continual dangers," the possession of one's freedom and property there being "very uncertain, and constantly exposed to the Invasion of others." The cause of this uncertainty, Locke holds, is that "the greater part" of men are "no strict observers of Equity and Justice." Specifically, the law of nature, though "plain and intelligible to all rational Creatures," is nevertheless inadequate to direct the actions of men to justice because they are generally "biassed by their Interest" and "partial to themselves." By the law of nature men are obliged not to harm others in their rights, and in fact to defend the rights of others against the unjust actions of wrongdoers; but by their own nature men are not much inclined to fulfill these duties.[22]

Thus, although Locke at times insists on the decidedly non-Hobbesian notion that man is by nature a sociable creature bound by the law of nature to respect the rights of others, it is in the end difficult to see that there is any *practical* difference between his understanding of the state of nature and that of Hobbes. For Hobbes, recall, men are by nature in an utterly lawless posture toward each other, all being equally authorized to destroy each other in the pursuit of their own interests: all men by nature have a right to all things, even one another's bodies or lives. Locke contends instead that men are by nature in a prepolitical state in which they are obliged to respect each other's rights to life, liberty, and estate. Nevertheless, Locke notes that when one man disregards the law of nature and uses force to threaten the life or freedom of another, they enter a state of war. In this state, Locke contends, the victim of aggression has a right to "destroy the other whenever he can, until the aggressor offers Peace, and desires reconciliation on such Terms, as may repair any wrongs he has already done, and secure the innocent for the future."[23] At the same time, however, Locke states, as we have seen, an apparently unqualified right, and even duty, of each man to preserve himself and hence to defend his own life against those who would destroy it. Presumably this duty applies even to those who are guilty of unjust aggression.[24] Thus on the understanding implied by Locke's account, while no one has a right to initiate a state of war, once one comes about both victim and aggressor equally have the right to destroy the other in order to preserve themselves. Yet, given Locke's account of the selfish inclinations of human nature, and more specifically his admission that in the state of nature man's "Freedom" is "constantly exposed to the invasion of others," we can only conclude that Locke's teaching implies that in the state of nature most men are in a state of war most of the time. That is to say, most men in Locke's state of nature are in a relationship in which there is no principle of justice that can regulate their actions toward each other. For most must either be victim or aggressor (or perhaps both in relation to different people), and both victim and aggressor seem to have a right to do what is necessary to preserve themselves, hence a right even to each other's bodies or lives. But, as we have seen, this is precisely the position of all men in Hobbes's state of nature.

The practical similarity of Hobbes' and Locke's understandings of the state of nature is also illuminated by reflecting on Locke's argument that in the state of nature each man is authorized to execute the law of nature. This individual right of enforcement, he contends, is necessary to ensure that the law of nature be observed. "For the *Law of Nature* would, as all other Laws that concern Men in this World, be in vain, if there were no body in the State of Nature, had a *Power to Execute* that Law, and thereby preserve the innocent and restrain offenders."[25] Nevertheless, as we have seen, subsequent passages in the *Second Treatise* clearly indicate that in the state of nature the law of nature is so uncertainly obeyed that the freedom and estate of men are in constant peril. Thus the law of nature on its own does not seem to "preserve the innocent and restrain offenders." Locke's argument, taken in its entirety, implies that the law of nature is vain. Yet if the law of nature exists but is powerless to govern the actions of men, or is able only minimally to influence them, then the Lockean state of nature is, again, practically Hobbesian.

It is worth noting in this context that in at least one passage Locke even seems to suggest a theoretical agreement with Hobbes with regard to one aspect of the question of the status of the law of nature. Recall that while Hobbes adopts the language of natural law, his teaching makes clear that he does not speak of a law of nature rooted in an eternal and transcendent order of things. At one point Locke seems to concur. Human beings need to establish written laws and political and judicial authorities to enforce and interpret them, he contends, for "the Law of Nature being unwritten, and so no where to be found but in the minds of Men, they who through Passion or Interest shall mis-cite, or misapply it, cannot so easily be convinced of their mistake where there is no establish'd Judge."[26] It is somewhat strange for a writer who insists that there is a divine basis for the law of nature also to suggest that, absent governmental codification, it exists only in the human mind. Be that as it may, in light of the practical similarities between the Lockean and Hobbesian accounts of the state of nature it is perhaps no surprise that Locke chooses the same expression as Hobbes to sum up his evaluation of it. For both men, it seems, man is by nature in an "ill condition."[27]

Locke's Hobbesian understanding of man as fundamentally self-interested and individualistic is also evident in his account of the transition from the state of nature to civil society. Men, Locke suggests, are not so much drawn into society by a desire for human fellowship as they are "driven into Society" by the "inconveniencies" of the state of nature, especially the insecurity of their lives and properties.[28] Moreover, for Locke, as for Hobbes, the establishment of civil society is not brought about by public-spirited motives. That is, while the aim of the legislative power is the *"preservation of the Society"* as a whole, yet individuals consent to the establishment of that power not so much for the security of all as for the security of their own individual interests. Men "enter into Society," Locke contends, "only with an intention in every one the better to preserve himself his Liberty and Property."[29] Even Locke's initial formulation of the law of nature, with its emphasis on man's duty to preserve *all* human life, implies that self-interest is the basic ground of human nature; for the obligation to humanity is qualified by a more fundamental obligation to oneself. Locke holds that each man is bound to do "as much as he can, to preserve the rest of Mankind," only so long as "his own Preservation comes not into competition" with theirs.[30] The implication that self-interest is foundational in Locke's account of human nature is confirmed and heightened later in the argument, when he speaks of "Self-Preservation" as the "Fundamental, Sacred, and unalterable Law for which" men "entered into Society."[31]

Locke's placement of self-interest at the core of human nature carries far-reaching and, on John Paul II's account, deeply problematic implications. To begin with, such an understanding implies that reason must be in the service of self-interest. That is, it implicitly reduces reason's role in human life to one of mere egotistic calculation. Moreover, Locke's constant emphasis on life and estate or property implies that self-interest is to be understood materialistically. On this view, reason is subservient to the human desire for life and physical ease, a position that is remarkably close to Hobbes's insistence that reason is only a scout and spy for the passions. Indeed, Locke appears not to seek to evade such implications but to affirm them openly. "God," he writes, has given men "reason to make use of it to the best advantage of life, and convenience."[32] For John Paul II, reason, a distinctively human capacity, looks to human perfection: it discerns the commands of the moral law, which are themselves intrinsically good and the path of man's completion in virtue and happiness, and which accordingly harmonize respect and care for others with each man's deepest well-being. In contrast, for both Locke and Hobbes reason is demoted to being in the service of purposes that are less elevated and more simply self-interested, and in fact ultimately indistinguishable from the aspirations of animals.

In Locke's account as in Hobbes's, this demotion of the distinctively human capacity is accompanied by a diminution in the human vocation. In Locke's initial statement of the law of nature, he indicates that it governs not only man's treatment of himself and other human beings, but also his use of the other living things of the earth. According to the law of nature, man "has not Liberty to destroy himself, or so much as any Creature in his Possession, but where some nobler use, than its bare Preservation calls for it."[33] This formulation raises the question: what is this "nobler use" to which we are to put the things of the earth and which can therefore justify their destruction? Elsewhere in the *Two Treatises* Locke provides an answer, and it is an answer that would seem to obliterate "the noble" as it had been understood in the premodern tradition of political philosophy. For the "nobler" use that legitimizes the destruction of other creatures turns out to be nothing greater than men's pursuit of "the comfortable preservation of their Beings." "Property," Locke argues, derives "from the Right a Man has to use any of the Inferior Creatures, for the Subsistence and Comfort of his Life," such that "he may even destroy the thing, that he has Property in by his use of it, where need requires."[34] In sum, Locke holds that the "Earth, and all that is therein, is given to Men for the Support and Comfort of their being"; but it would seem difficult to distinguish this from the view that man has no business in the world higher than seeing to his comfort and preservation.[35]

One might contend in Locke's defense that he does not so much deny the existence and importance of a higher human calling as he neglects it, and that he neglects it properly, with a view to the aim of his political teaching. After all, one can believe that human beings perfect their nature and achieve their highest happiness through observance of the moral law and the gift of self, and yet remain silent on these matters in a political treatise because one holds that politics is not properly concerned with them. In response, we might observe that the highest human activities do not ordinarily flourish spontaneously, that they require cultivation, and that therefore even mere neglect of them may well result in a loss of the sense of their importance. On this view, the propagation of an incomplete account of human life and ends, like that found in the *Two Treatises*, will result not just in an incomplete education but a miseducation regarding these issues.

Moreover, a political teaching that prescinds from man's loftier moral purposes will tend implicitly to subordinate those purposes to whatever it posits as the aim of the political community. Despite their often disdainful attitude toward those entrusted with political authority, human beings sense that this authority itself is somehow awesome and venerable, that it is the guardian of the community's dearest interests.

It is therefore difficult for us to think (neutrally) of some matters as beyond government's scope without also thinking (normatively) that they are also beneath its notice. Simply put, it is difficult to privatize a matter without also in some measure trivializing it. Thus a teaching that seeks to limit politics to a concern with the conditions of comfortable self-preservation will incline in effect to subordinate man's moral excellence to his bodily ease.

Whether or not this tendency is necessary and unavoidable, it is certainly one to which Locke's teaching is prone. Locke contends that men entered into civil society "only" for the sake of "*Safety and Security*" and accordingly that "Government has no other end but the preservation of Property," understood as life, liberty, and estate. He also holds, however, that government—or, more specifically, its legislative authority—is the "Supream Power" in the society, "to which all the rest are and must be subordinate." Locke elsewhere states that "all the *Obedience*, which by the most solemn Ties any one can be obliged to pay, ultimately terminates in this *Supream Power*, and is directed by those Laws which it enacts." Locke does not deny the existence of other institutions—like families and churches—that may serve more elevated ends than comfortable self-preservation. Nevertheless, his teaching subordinates such institutions to that institution concerned only with securing the conditions of comfortable self-preservation. Thus, even if he recognizes a higher end for man, Locke's teaching subordinates the institutions responsible for it to the institution responsible for lower ends. It is hard not to draw from such principles the conclusion that comfortable self-preservation is ultimately a more serious consideration than moral excellence. At all events, Locke invites his reader to this conclusion with the heightened rhetoric characterizing self-preservation as a "Fundamental, Sacred, and unalterable Law."[36]

LOCKE'S TEACHING AND RESPECT FOR LIFE

As we have just seen, a powerful streak of hedonistic self-interest runs through Locke's anthropology. Indeed, Locke appears to treat the desire for comfortable self-preservation as the most powerful element in human nature and hence as the fundamental principle of his natural law. As we have also seen, however, John Paul II's argument holds that such hedonism tends to undermine a principled respect for human life by diminishing its value to a matter of utilitarian calculus. Such effects are evident in certain aspects of Locke's political teaching.

A kind of lack of reverence for human life appears most obviously in Locke's account of the status of those who seriously violate the law of nature. In the state of nature, Locke contends, the life of a murderer, or indeed of anyone who uses force against another with a view to taking the latter's property, is forfeit. Anyone may kill such a man. Such wrongdoers have "renounced Reason, the common Rule and Measure, God hath given to Mankind" and "therefore may be destroyed" like lions or tigers or any of the "wild Savage Beasts, with whom Men can have no society."[37]

What is striking about Locke's teaching here is not its suggestion that one may in some cases kill those guilty of such crimes. Such a teaching is consistent with a longstanding Catholic tradition of legitimate self-defense and just punishment, and therefore it cannot easily be understood as a moral error characteristic of the emerging culture of death that John Paul II criticizes. Of course, John Paul II is famously critical of the death penalty in *Evangelium Vitae,* and his criticism's tension with the earlier Catholic acceptance of capital punishment has generated a controversy of competing interpretations of his intention.[38] Some contend that his denunciation of capital punishment is best understood merely as a prudential argument that such punishment, though in principle morally legitimate, need not and ought not be applied in our present cultural circumstances. Others view the death-penalty passages in *Evangelium Vitae* as suggesting a principled rejection of capital punishment that represents a new development in Catholic doctrine. Wherever the truth lies in this debate, however, is beside the present point. For even apart from the question of the legitimacy or appropriateness of the death penalty, it is clear that Locke's teaching on this matter gives expression to a morality wholly alien to that informing the pope's argument in *Evangelium Vitae.* Locke actually suggests that murderers, and generally those who resort unjustly to force, have renounced their humanity and may be treated as wild animals. Such a trespasser against the law of nature revolts "from his own kind to that of Beasts" and so is liable to be "destroied by the injur'd person and the rest of mankind . . . as any other wild beast, or noxious brute with whom Mankind can have neither Society nor Security."[39] While John Paul II does not directly address the question of the moral status of the serious wrongdoer in *Evangelium Vitae*, it is clear that his understanding of human life forecloses such a teaching as Locke's. For John Paul II the human being as such deserves a certain respect because of a dignity that inheres in his very nature, in his creation in the image and likeness of God and his lofty vocation to communion with God through gift of self according to the moral law. A murderer damages his dignity and deserves to be punished, but he cannot be said to renounce his humanity and all claim to the respect of others. Yet this is precisely what Locke suggests.

For John Paul II, respect for the dignity of the human person is an unconditional demand of the moral law. For Locke, however, such respect can be forfeited and therefore is conditional. It is, in fact, conditional upon the life in question's bearing upon the security of others. That is to say, respect for the dignity of another is not absolutely obligatory but is dependent on how that other's life relates to one's own fundamental self-interest in self-preservation. For John Paul II, the fundamental consideration in dealing with a murderer will be the moral law and ultimately the law of love. Thus one's treatment of the murderer will take into account the need to punish him consistent with the possibility of his reformation, consistent with the moral well-being of his fellow citizens (that is, without fostering in them feelings of hatred), and consistent with the protection against unjust aggression that his fellow citizens deserve and justice demands. In contrast, for Locke the fundamental consideration in dealing with a murderer would appear to be the desire for self-preservation. While John Paul II might risk a certain lenity with a view to fostering repentance in the criminal or avoiding blood-lust in the community, precisely because one's physical safety is not the ultimate moral criterion, there is in contrast a clear sense in Locke that one's safety is just too urgent to take any such chances in one's dealing with such an evildoer. Thus does the elevation of comfortable self-preservation begin to erode respect for human life in Locke's teaching.

One might question whether this issue presents a real difference between Locke and the Christian tradition that John Paul II represents. After all, Locke appeals not only to a concern with safety but also to biblical authority in his discussion of how a murderer is to be treated. *"Who so sheddeth Mans Blood, by Man shall his Blood be shed,"* Locke notes, referring to this passage from Genesis as a "great Law of Nature." He further appeals to the Biblical account of the first homocide as supporting his view that the murderer's life is forfeit: "And Cain was so fully convinced, that every one had a Right to destroy such a Criminal, that after the Murther of his Brother, he cries out, Every one that findeth me, shall slay me; so plain was it writ in the Hearts of all Mankind."[40] It would appear, however, that Locke is selectively relying on scripture to confirm a position that he has already reached on grounds of mere material self-interest. For while the Bible does endorse capital punishment for murderers, it is surely far from suggesting that they have renounced their humanity and all claims upon the respect of others. Indeed, Locke's selectivity is evident even in his appropriation of the story of Cain and Abel. The remark on which Locke relies is part of Cain's conversation with God, a conversation in which God responds as follows to Cain's fear that all will slay him: "Not so! If anyone slays Cain, vengeance shall be taken on him sevenfold."[41] Locke omits God's rejoinder, and by doing so he creates a false impression of harmony between Biblical morality and his understanding of the law of nature. In contrast to Locke's teaching, in the Bible God does not completely withdraw his protection from a murderer, even from one guilty of malicious and premeditated fratricide.

Although Locke's law of nature allows, it does not absolutely require, that a murderer be killed: slavery is a permissible substitute for death in such a case. When a man has "forfeited his own Life, by some Act that deserves Death, he, to whom he has forfeited it, may (when he has him in his Power) delay to take it, and make use of him to his own Service." Such bondage, Locke continues, does the enslaved wrongdoer "no injury," for "whenever he finds the hardship of his Slavery out-weigh the value of his Life, 'tis in his Power, by resisting the Will of his Master, to draw on himself the Death he desires."[42] Apparently it can be consistent with Locke's law of nature for one to desire one's own death and indirectly to cause it. Here again, then, we find in Locke's teaching what John Paul II would surely consider a problematic devaluation of human life.

The present point does not depend on the claim that Locke is here advocating a right to suicide. Indeed, earlier in this very passage Locke seems to forbid suicide by stating that man has no "Power" to "take away his own life," which echoes his claims, in his foundational statement of the law of nature, that man "is bound to preserve himself" and "has not liberty to destroy himself."[43] For the moment, then, let us grant Locke's apparent position that intending to provoke one's own killing does not necessarily amount to self-destruction in violation of the law of nature. Nevertheless, the motivation Locke posits as justifying such an action reveals a sense of what makes life valuable that departs radically from that affirmed by John Paul II. Locke indicates, after all, that hardship can outweigh the value of a human life to its possessor. Although he does not specify, we are drawn—especially by Locke's suggestions elsewhere that the human calling is summed up in the quest for *comfortable* self-preservation—to the conclusion that Locke has in mind material hardship. Such notions are, of course, utterly alien to the argument of *Evangelium Vitae*, and are in fact explicitly rejected by it both as false and as tending to establish the cultural conditions under which the destruction of innocent life, even of one's own life, will appear desirable in some circumstances.

To be sure, to claim that something is desirable is not the same as to claim that it is right, a point that Locke seems to underscore with his repeated assertions that a man has no liberty to destroy himself. Thus it would seem strange to speak of a right to suicide in Locke. Nevertheless, such a right can be said to be an implication of his teaching, or at least of one strand of his teaching. For Locke to some extent embraces the Hobbesian reduction of right to desire, thus opening the door to all of its calamitous consequences.

In the *First Treatise*, Locke contends that the "Foundation of a right to the Creatures, for the particular support and use of each individual Person himself," is the desire for "Self-preservation," the "first and strongest desire God Planted in Men, and wrought into the very Principles of their Nature."[44] That is, the right to the means of self-preservation— and we surely are to conclude the right to self-preservation itself—is grounded in the desire for self-preservation. For Locke, as for Hobbes, then, our most important rights must be understood as based upon our most important desires. But since, as Hobbes observes, the desires are variable, we must suspect that the rights to which they give rise are similarly variable. What, then, becomes of the right to self-preservation—and the obligation to care for one's preservation—when the desire for self-preservation wanes or fails, as it does in some cases? Or, to put the question more forcefully, if rights are based on desires—as Locke teaches in the *First Treatise*—then how can we avoid the conclusion that hardships that render death desirable—as in the case of the slave mentioned in the *Second Treatise*—also render it a right? Thus does Locke's teaching incline in the direction of a right to suicide.[45]

There is more, for the passage in question suggests not only that our obligations to ourselves, but also our obligations to others, depend fundamentally upon our desires. Locke's argument that the right to self-preservation depends on the desire for self-preservation is made in the context of an inquiry into why children come to possess the property of their parents when the parents die. The "ground" of this practice, he contends, is another deeply rooted desire. While men's first and strongest desire is for their own preservation, "next to this, God Planted in Men a strong desire also of propagating their Kind, and continuing themselves in their Posterity." This desire, he concludes, "gives Children a Title, to share in the *Property* of their Parents, and a Right to Inherit their Possessions." Men, he sums up, are "by a like Obligation bound to preserve what they have begotten, as to preserve themselves."[46] Thus, it seems, the obligation to preserve one's own children, like the obligation to preserve oneself, depends upon the natural desire to do it. Once again, then, we are led to suspect that the obligation must fail with the desire. Accordingly, this strand of Locke's teaching tends to erode the force of his many pious pronouncements, noted earlier, about the duty of parents to nourish their children.

One might respond that this concern is more theoretical than practical: since most human beings do in fact feel a strong desire to care for their children, the rights of children are likely to be secure. Nevertheless, it cannot be dismissed as completely theoretical, since we know from experience that in some parents, few though they may be, these feelings are weak; and indeed in some cases the parental feelings are so debilitated or disordered as to lead to a deadly neglect or even outright murder. By following Hobbes's effort to establish justice only on the desires, Locke's teaching undermines any objective basis on which we might disapprove of such feelings and behaviors.[47] On Locke's teaching, moreover, rights will be most vulnerable in the case of children who have little hold upon adult affections, those who are least able to induce feelings of obligation in their parents. This is the case most emphatically, of course, with the unborn, who have not yet begun to establish the bonds of love that come from interacting face to face with parents. We now know from experience, moreover, that many people—especially those formed by a culture that tends to venerate Lockean comfortable self-preservation— are capable of demanding and acting upon a right to destroy their own unborn children. There seems to be nothing solid in Locke's teaching to forbid this, and indeed much that would appear to invite it.

THE LOCKEAN OPENING TO TYRANNY

According to John Paul II's argument in *Evangelium Vitae*, when hedonism and materialism—as well as their offspring, suicide and abortion— are at hand, tyranny cannot be far behind. We have seen, however, that Locke's teaching includes elements of a Hobbesian anthropology that undermine a sound basis for respect for human dignity and accordingly open the door to an affirmation of suicide and abortion. We are led to wonder, then, whether Locke's account contains evidence of the opening to tyranny that the pope thinks is characteristic of such a teaching.

To begin with, Locke's teaching suggests that one may—even that one should—cooperate with a tyrant—even to the point of carrying out his most wicked commands—if doing so is necessary to preserve one's own life. There is a great silence in Locke's teaching. Unlike John Paul II, who expressly teaches that it may be necessary to embrace martyrdom in order to witness to the inviolable holiness of the moral law and the dignity of the human person, Locke never raises the case in which obedience to the moral law requires one to sacrifice one's life by refusing to perform some grave injustice.[48] On the contrary, Locke indicates that there can be no such obligation, because for him there is something more holy than any obligation to avoid doing injustice to others. "Self-Preservation," we recall, is for Locke the "Fundamental, Sacred, and unalterable Law."[49] There is thus no basis in Locke for disapproving the choice of the man who, for example, decides to operate the gas chamber rather than be executed himself.

From here it is but a short step to tolerating tyranny over others for the sake of one's own self-interest, understood not necessarily as self-preservation but merely as convenience or comfort. Locke, as we have seen, suggests that human obligations are based upon human desires. He also indicates that human beings are fundamentally self-interested. It is difficult to see, then, on what basis the unmolested subjects of a tyrannical government could be moved to imperil their own positions by interceding on behalf of their less fortunate fellows. Certainly Locke neither expects nor encourages such behavior. After all, he indicates that men, being fundamentally self-interested, enter into civil society for the security of their own rights, and not those of others. Thus one cannot not expect them to believe that their government is seriously amiss so long as it threatens others' rights and not their own. Accordingly, in his discussion of the right to resist a tyranny Locke indicates that such resistance will only come if the government's acts touch the "majority of the people," or at least "light only on some few, but in such Cases, as the Precedent, and Consequences seem to threaten all."[50] For the Lockean man, tyranny is evil only in relation to his own rights and interests, and hence may not be evil at all so long as these are secure.

Will the Lockean man go so far as to foster tyranny willingly and actively for the sake of advancing his own interests? We can give only an ambiguous answer to this question. On the one hand, as we have seen, many formulations of Locke's law of nature—presenting others as God's property, not our own, to be preserved to the extent that we can—seem to forbid such exploitation. On the other hand, passages that appear to base obligations upon desires, along with those that present man as fundamentally self-interested, cannot but lead us to think that a willingness to tyrannize others can be reasonable if it advances our interests. Of course, Locke might well warn those who are so disposed that any effort to use government to exploit others may result in resistance, and that such resistance might lead to a dissolution of the society, or even to the would-be exploiter's enslavement by his intended prey. Thus Lockean man might well conclude that in most cases justice is the best policy. Such a conclusion, however, depends entirely upon a selfish calculation of one's own material interests, and therefore will always leave the weakest members of the community exposed to tyranny at the hands of the strongest. Thus the Lockean man's approach to justice contains the same openness to tyranny that John Paul II attributes to the materialistic "culture of death" and that is evident with even more clarity in the teaching of Hobbes.[51]

CONCLUSION

Such are the grave consequences that follow from Locke's teaching. Rather, we should say, more precisely, that these consequences follow from some elements of his teaching. For in opposition to such elements, and forbidding such consequences, stand Locke's various statements, noted in the first part of this chapter, of an objective law of nature rooted in the will of God. *The Two Treatises*, it would seem, contain two Lockes. On the one hand, there is the theistic Locke, who strides forward to occupy center stage in the most general articulation of the law of nature in section 6 of the *Second Treatise*. This Locke's words appear to inform many of the moral judgments in the *Two Treatises*. On the other hand, a Hobbesian Locke seems to peer furtively through many other passages, pushing, as we have also seen, Locke's teaching toward some dangerously Hobbesian conclusions. These two Lockes, which exist in tension with one another, are a cause of much scholarly perplexity. How do these different strains relate to each other? Can they be successfully harmonized? Is Locke remarkably subtle or simply incoherent? His stature forbids the second alternative, and so scholars have tended to dispute over which Locke is the real Locke. This dispute, however, is perhaps beside our purpose, for we can at least say the following about Locke from the standpoint of John Paul II. Despite the apparent wholesomeness of his theistic presentations of natural law, the Hobbesian elements of Locke's anthropology compromise that natural law in its consistency and force, thus creating—whether intentionally or not—an opening in Locke's political teaching to the "culture of death" and its most distressing consequences.

Chapter 5

HUME AND THE MORALITY OF SYMPATHY

Hobbes and Locke must be regarded as two of the key intellectual architects of liberal modernity. Their teachings, however, appear to advance precisely those strains of thought of which John Paul II is so critical in *Evangelium Vitae*. As we have seen, Hobbes openly embraces, and Locke at least opens the door to, the kind of hedonistic individualism that the pope believes undermines respect for human dignity and human rights. To this extent it would appear that the defects of contemporary culture that the pope observes are rooted in the theoretical foundations of modernity itself.

There are, however, other versions of liberal modernity, ones that may avoid the problematic aspects of Hobbesian and Lockean political theory. Here we may think especially of the Scottish Enlightenment, which seems to repudiate the hedonistic individualism characteristic of earlier modern thought. Where Hobbes and Locke emphasize man's supposed natural isolation from his fellows and accordingly seek to erect moral and political principles on the basis of self-interested calculation, the thinkers of the Scottish Enlightenment hold that man is naturally sociable and that morality is rooted in a natural human sympathy. Such a teaching would seem to go some way toward correcting the aspects of the Hobbesian and Lockean anthropology that John Paul II finds so dangerously erroneous and thus possibly points the way to a modernity secured against the erosion of rights. With a view to exploring this possibility, we turn to the thought of David Hume, one of the leading figures of the Scottish Enlightenment, and in particular to his argument in the *Enquiry Concerning the Principles of Morals*.

HUME'S WORLDLY PHILOSOPHY

Before considering how Hume departs from and corrects his early modern predecessors, we may observe that in some respects his teaching follows the same trail that they blazed. There is a certain worldliness, for lack of a better term, that characterizes the thought of Hobbes, Locke, and Hume, in contrast to the preoccupation with the transcendent we find in John Paul II and the Aristotelian-Thomistic tradition on which he draws. Hume did not escape—nor, for that matter, did he seek to escape—the long reach of Machiavelli's revolutionary realism any more than did Hobbes or Locke. Accordingly, there is no sense in Hume's ethical and political works that his teaching is oriented toward or informed by any notion of a transcendent supreme good for man. On the contrary, he insists on a much more down to earth "experimental" approach to morality, one that takes its bearings from the observable realities of everyday human experience. "Men," Hume argues, "are now cured of their passion for hypotheses and systems in natural philosophy, and will hearken to no arguments but those which are derived from experience." "It is," he continues, "full time they should attempt a like reformation in all moral disquisitions; and reject every system of ethics . . . which is not founded on fact and observation."[1] It is difficult to read this passage without calling to mind—and discerning the influence of—Machiavelli's similar determination in *The Prince* to take his bearings not from "that which ought to be done" according to teachings derived from "imagined republics and principalities" but instead from "that which is done" in fact, or according to the "effectual truth."[2] Animated by this spirit, Hume writes dismissively of the union of ethical philosophy with "theology," which, he suggests, "bends every branch of knowledge to its own purpose, without much regard to the phaenomena of nature, or to the unbiassed sentiments of the mind," warping thought and speech from their "natural course."[3]

In the absence of transcendence, Humean man takes on a humble stature reminiscent of his Hobbesian predecessor. No longer understood as a being uniquely created in the image and likeness of a transcendent God, man is denied the God-like powers of wisdom and freedom attributed to him by the older tradition to which John Paul II gives contemporary utterance. Hence we find Hume reiterating Hobbes's rejection of free will and his insistence on the subordination of reason to passion. The human sensation of free will, Hume suggests in his *A Treatise of Human Nature*, is illusory, the "operations of the mind" being determined by "necessity" no less than the "actions of matter."[4] Reason, he further contends, "can never produce any action, or give rise to volition," and is equally "incapable" on the other side of "preventing volition, or of disputing the preference with any passion or emotion." He concludes, in terms recalling the *Leviathan*, that "[r]eason is, and ought only to be the slave of the passions, and can never pretend to any other office than to serve and obey them."[5]

Finally, for Hume as for Hobbes, the lowered status of human nature points to a lower origin for human morality. No longer a path to transcendence and perfection, morality becomes nothing more than a manifestation of the passions—as, indeed, seems inevitable, given reason's subjection to desire. According to the "hypothesis" Hume embraces, "morality is determined by sentiment."[6] The "moral obligation of duty," he suggests elsewhere, arises from "the necessary course of the passions and sentiments."[7]

SOCIABILITY, SYMPATHY, AND THE MORAL SENSE

While Hume follows Hobbes in basing morality on the passions, however, he understands the human passions differently, and he accordingly departs from Hobbes's account of the relationship of morality to human nature. Hobbes, recall, posits a kind of moral relativism arising from the inconstancy of passion. Our notions of good and evil, he insists, are determined by our passions, by our desires and aversions; yet these passions differ so greatly from man to man, and even within each man from time to time, that there can be no common moral law that exists by nature. Rather, morality, the laws of nature, must be artificially devised by men in order to escape the disastrous lawlessness of their natural condition.

In contrast, Hume forthrightly rejects such relativism. For him, those "who have denied" the "reality" of commonly perceived "moral distinctions" are "disingenuous disputants" who cannot really believe the position they defend. Even the most insensible man, Hume argues, "must often be touched by the images of RIGHT and WRONG" and discern that "others are susceptible of like impressions."[8] Hume is aware of the Hobbesian notion that morality is entirely artificial. He speaks of those "skeptics, both ancient and modern," who have "inferred" from the "usefulness of the social virtues" that they are completely "invented" by "the art of politicians, in order to render men more tractable, and subdue their natural ferocity and selfishness, which incapacitated them for society." Nevertheless, Hume holds that moral distinctions must have some basis in nature, for if they were wholly the product of artifice their inventors would never have been able to make them intelligible to others. He thus concludes that "moral affection" and "dislike" are "founded on the original constitution of the human mind," that our judgments of good and evil are not, as Hobbes would have it, radically subjective, but rather arise from "some internal sense or feeling, which nature has made universal in the whole species."[9]

For Hume, the passions upon which morality is based are not only more uniform but also more generous than was believed by his early modern predecessors, who, as we have seen, derive moral obligation from individual self-interest, which they take to be the most powerful force in human nature. Hume names Hobbes and Locke as being among those "moderns" who "maintained the selfish system of morals," according to which, he elsewhere indicates, each man esteems virtue only with a view to his own "self-love" and "private interest," which depend on the "order in society" that virtue sustains.[10] Hume, however, seeks to distinguish his account from this "selfish theory," which, he contends, is opposed by "the voice of nature and experience." After all, he argues, human beings often praise acts of virtue performed in the distant past or in far away lands, where the most subtle "imagination would not discover any appearance of self-interest" or find any relationship to "our present happiness and security." Moreover, he adds, the courageous deed of an adversary "commands our approbation" even though "in its consequences it may be acknowledged prejudicial to our particular interest."[11] The basis of morality, then, is not for Hume reducible to individual self-interest but must be based on "a more public affection" which interests us in the well-being of society itself.[12] In sum, while Hobbes contends that nature renders man utterly isolated, Hume holds that "[m]an is a sociable . . . being."[13] As a result, Hume finds that morality is directly rooted in human nature, while Hobbes presents it as an artificial creation of self-interested calculation.

The root of human sociability and morality is, according to Hume, man's natural capacity for sympathy or humanity, his ability spontaneously to experience the feelings of his fellow human beings. It appears to Hume that "all the affections readily pass from one person to another, and beget correspondent movements in every human creature." Whenever one sees the effects of passion in another's actions, one's mind immediately forms an impression of the passion animating the other, and this impression is quickly "converted into the passion itself" in the observer.[14] Thus, Hume observes, "wherever we go, whatever we reflect on or converse about, every thing still presents us with the view of human happiness or misery, and excites in our breast a sympathetic movement of pleasure or uneasiness." He accordingly concludes that "humanity or fellow-feeling with others" is "a principle in human nature."[15]

According to Hume, our sympathy or humanity is the basis of our natural obligation to observe justice and the other social virtues, or those virtues that pertain to our obligations to respect the rights and well being of others. Hume concedes, and even emphasizes, the utility of such virtues, the role they play in sustaining a stable social environment in which each individual's material well being will be secured. Nevertheless, unlike Hobbes, Hume does not draw the conclusion that the social virtues are therefore approved and observed by individuals only on the basis of self-interested calculation. Rather, he notes that our natural sympathy leads us spontaneously to approve whatever we understand to be useful to our fellow beings, and hence to feel a natural esteem for justice. The "principles of humanity," Hume contends, have sufficient "authority over our sentiments" to "give us a general approbation of what is useful to society, and blame of what is dangerous or pernicious." Thus the "merit" attributed "to the social virtues," he concludes, "arises chiefly from that regard, which the natural sentiment of benevolence engages us to pay to the interests of mankind and society."[16]

As a result of such considerations, Hume can affirm the goodness of justice in a way that Hobbes cannot. For Hobbes, the natural passions of human beings are radically self-interested. The quest to satisfy these passions, however, leads to a state of war in which they cannot be satisfied. Human beings accordingly embrace justice as a kind of truce, establishing the peaceful conditions under which at least some of their desires may be fulfilled. On this view, justice is utterly artificial and good only instrumentally. Men have no natural desire to respect the rights of others, but they agree to do so as a way of protecting their own individual interests. Thus Hobbes claims that earlier thinkers have erred in believing the moral virtues to be good in themselves: they are in fact nothing more than the "meanes of peaceable, sociable, and comfortable living."[17] For Hume, in contrast, there is an element of sociability in human nature, a natural sympathy that interests man in the well-being of his fellows. Accordingly, justice and the other sociable virtues have a direct foothold in the passions. Thus for Humean man justice, or doing right by others, can be experienced as good intrinsically and not only instrumentally. Because of the operations of sympathy, Hume contends, the "social virtues" possess "a natural beauty and amiableness, which, at first, antecedent to all precept or education, recommends them to the esteem of mankind, and engages their affections." Unlike Hobbes, then, Hume finds "virtue" to be "an end" and "desirable on its own account, without fee or reward, merely for the immediate satisfaction which it conveys."[18]

SYMPATHY AND SELF-INTEREST

In light of the preceding argument, it would seem that Hume's account falls short of what John Paul II thinks is necessary to sustain respect for human rights and human dignity, yet without embracing, and perhaps even introducing a corrective to, the hedonistic individualism of Hobbes. On the one hand, from the standpoint of *Evangelium Vitae*'s argument, Hume does not establish justice on a secure foundation precisely because he excludes the transcendent from his teaching. For the pope, human dignity is sufficiently established only when we recognize that each human life is an image and likeness of God and consequently possesses an objective value. In the absence of such a belief, John Paul II suggests, we begin to view the lives of others as valuable only in relation to ourselves, which is the first step toward the tyrannical subordination of their rights to our own interests. Yet the notion that human life has a transcendent and objective value is no less alien to Hume than to Hobbes: for both thinkers the lives of others have value only in relation to our own feelings or passions.

On the other hand, however, Hume's understanding of the passions is, as we have seen, more generous than Hobbes's. Hobbesian man's estimate of another's value necessarily involves an element of selfish calculation. This would not seem to be the case for Hume, however, because for him man's natural passions are not exclusively self-interested but also somewhat sociable. For Hume our natural sociability spontaneously attaches us to our fellows and enables us to make their interests our own. By our capacity for sympathy we can feel as they feel, and hence value as they value, and therefore value them as we value ourselves. Put another way, on Hume's account our natural sympathy ensures that we can experience virtue, or behavior looking to the well-being of others, not merely as a means to other ends but as an end in itself. Thus for Hume, unlike for Hobbes, the moral law need not be understood as what John Paul II calls a heteronomy, a set of rules imposed from outside human nature, but instead as responding to and fulfilling our nature. Hume's teaching therefore seems to avoid the problem of heteronomous moralities that John Paul II identifies: by separating the moral law from man's natural good, they create an inclination to evade the requirements of the moral law when its observation does not advance our own interests. Perhaps, then, John Paul II is incorrect to contend that human life must be understood in relation to the life of God if it is to be properly valued. Perhaps Hume's teaching demonstrates that respect for human rights and human dignity requires no theological foundation, only an adequate account of the human passions. Perhaps, then, there is a philosophic version of liberal modernity that, unlike those offered by Hobbes and Locke, is proof against the erosion of respect for justice that the pope finds characteristic of contemporary society.

A fuller examination of Hume's teaching reveals, however, that, despite these promising elements, it tends, in the end, to the same deterioration of respect for human dignity and human rights that John Paul II finds in contemporary society and that we have also found to be characteristic of the thought of Hobbes and Locke. Hume can affirm the natural goodness of justice because he presents it as directly rooted in a natural human passion, sympathy. Nevertheless, Hume offers at best an equivocal support for justice, because on his account our humanity includes other passions that undermine our commitment to justice. Hume contends that "we are always inclined, from our natural philanthropy, to give preference to the happiness of society, and consequently to virtue, above its opposite." He includes with this remark, however, the following pivotal qualification: "*where interest or revenge or envy perverts not our disposition.*"[19] He elsewhere concedes, however, that such morally problematic passions are just as natural as our philanthropy or "benevolence."[20] Hume seeks, as we have noted before, to establish his moral teaching on our experience of the observable aspects of human nature. Yet those aspects cannot give unmixed approval to the moral good.

Indeed, Hume at times concedes that the nonmoral elements in our nature are more powerful than the moral ones. The "sentiments" arising from the "general interests of the community," it seems, "in most men" are "not so strong as those, which have a reference to private good." Again: "Sympathy, we shall allow, is much fainter than our concern for ourselves, and sympathy with persons remote from us, much fainter than that with persons near and contiguous." None of this, to be sure, denies the reality of sympathy, which remains a force in human nature on the basis of which we can "form some general unalterable standard, by which we may approve or disapprove of characters and manners." Nevertheless, because of the natural strength of our amoral passions, "the heart takes not part entirely with these general notions, nor regulates all its love and hatred, by the universal, abstract differences of vice and virtue, without regard to self, or the persons with whom we are more intimately connected."[21] In sum, for Hume sympathy has enough power in our nature to render virtue agreeable to our general taste, but by no means enough reliably to govern our actions.[22] In the terms of John Paul II, then, Hume's moral teaching must be somewhat heteronomous. On Hume's account morality is certainly not alien to all of our natural desires, yet it remains alien to some of the most powerful ones. According to the pope, respect for human rights and human dignity is adequately assured only when men understand that the moral good is *the* authentic human good, for only then will they realize that they can never secure their genuine interests by doing injustice to each other. For Hume, however, the moral good is at best *a* true human good, one good among the several toward which our natural passions incline us. To the extent that Hume derives his moral teaching only from observable human nature, while at the same time admitting that self-interest is commonly more powerful than sympathy, on his account the moral good cannot claim to be the most authoritative of human goods. Thus it would seem that his argument establishes respect for human dignity and human rights on a very uncertain foundation.

Evaluated in light of *Evangelium Vitae*'s principles, Hume offers only a somewhat less impoverished version of liberal modernity's understanding of the good for man. For John Paul II, drawing on the tradition of classical and Catholic moral and political thought, man is a being of transcendent origins and destiny, whose supreme good is realized through works according to the moral law and finally through the gift of self to others. For Hobbes, man is just another soulless body in a soulless universe, whose good is no more than the selfish satisfaction of his own desires for life, pleasure, and power. Hume seeks to correct Hobbes's understanding of human nature, but in the end he goes no further than to offer a slight modification: man is not simply self-interested, but he is a fundamentally self-interested being whose self-interest is qualified by a natural but rather weak sociability and sympathy. Thus for Hume the good for man can be understood as little more than a kind of sociable materialism. Man is made not for love but for a genial selfishness. Hume never openly articulates such a diminished understanding of the good life, yet it is evident in a number of his passing remarks, perhaps most obviously in his condemnation of the "monkish virtues." According to Hume, "[c]elibacy, fasting, penance, mortification, self-denial, humility, silence, solitude, and the whole train of monkish virtues" are "every where rejected by men of sense" and must be denied the title of virtue, "because they serve no manner of purpose; neither advance a man's fortune in the world, nor render him a more valuable member of society; neither qualify him for the entertainment of company, nor encrease his power of self-enjoyment."[23] For Hume, it seems, man's purpose is exhausted by the pleasures of physical well-being and an undemanding gregariousness. Thus when he speaks of "happiness" it is presented less as the activity of the moral virtues than as the possession of such goods as the "prospect of elevation, advancement, a figure in life, prosperous success, a steady command over fortune, and the execution of great or advantageous undertakings," or as "ease, plenty, authority, and the gratification of every appetite."[24] In sum, while Hobbes understands the good as hedonistic individualism, Hume understands it as hedonistic sociability.[25]

From the standpoint of John Paul II, Hume's diminution of the human good is morally and politically problematic because it tends to erode a principled appreciation for the value of human life as human life. That is, while avoiding the single-minded materialism of Hobbes, Hume's account of the good, with its emphasis on both the self-interested and sociable pleasures, nevertheless introduces an element of utilitarianism into our judgments of the value of other human beings. For the Humean man, again, other human beings are valued only in relation to his own feelings and are not viewed as possessing an objective and transcendent value. Accordingly, in Hume's thought the combination of self-interested and sociable desires that dominates human nature becomes the standard by which the worth of human beings is measured. The inevitable result is that those who are of little use with a view to the satisfaction of such desires are taken to be of little or no worth. This becomes clear in Hume's discussion of the "fool," or what we today would call the mentally disabled person. According to Hume, because the fool is "totally incapacitated" for "[b]usiness, books," and "conversation," he is, apart from "drudgery" that he might perform, "a useless burden upon the earth." He continues:

> Except the affection of parents, the strongest and most indissoluble
> bond in nature, no connexion has strength sufficient to support the
> disgust arising from this character. Love itself, which can subsist

under treachery, ingratitude, malice, and infidelity, is immediately extinguished by it, when perceived and acknowledged; nor are deformity and old age more fatal to the dominion of that passion. So dreadful are the ideas of an utter incapacity for any purpose or undertaking, and of continued error and misconduct in life![26]

Hume's language here strikingly anticipates John Paul II's observation that a utilitarian culture will regard a life requiring "greater acceptance, love and care" as "useless" and "an intolerable burden."[27] We may also note that Hume's suggestion that the fool is a "useless burden" apart from his capacity for menial labor implies that a mentally *and* physically disabled person would be a "useless burden" without qualification. For Hume, man's good is to be found in the satisfaction of our self-interested and sociable desires; and therefore any human being who is neither productive nor socially engaging is to be judged worthless.

Furthermore, Hume's impoverished account of the good tends to undermine our commitment to the moral law, which is the safeguard of respect for human rights and human dignity. For Hume, insofar as our self-interested desires are the most powerful, their satisfaction will loom as the primary element in the human good. As a result, justice will be valued for the most part instrumentally. To be sure, as we have seen, justice does on Hume's understanding respond to our natural sympathy, and to that extent may be taken as naturally good. Nevertheless, given the predominance of our self-interested passions, sympathy will at best make justice appear good in the abstract, while when it comes to one's own actions the naturally good will appear as whatever advances one's interests. Justice sometimes secures self-interest but sometimes does not. It will therefore be valued only conditionally and will be abandoned when it appears to become useless.

Hume's utilitarian understanding of justice comes most clearly to light in his discussion of the most extreme cases. If a society were to fall into such privation that "the utmost frugality and industry" could not preserve the majority from death and the rest from "extreme misery," he argues, then justice could properly be abandoned, being displaced by "the stronger motives of necessity and self-preservation." The "use" of justice, after all, is "to procure happiness and security, by preserving order in society." Thus, in those cases in which the society is "ready to perish from extreme necessity, no greater evil can be dreaded from violence and injustice; and every man may now provide for himself by all the means, which prudence can dictate, or humanity permit."[28] Similarly, Hume contends that in war not only are the ordinary rules of justice abandoned, but even that all justice may be jettisoned. Rules of warfare may be posited and obeyed, so long as they remain advantageous through the common observance of both belligerent powers. If, however, a "civilized nation" is at war with "barbarians" who respect "no rules even of war," Hume contends, then "the former must also suspend their observance of them, where they no longer serve to any purpose; and must render every action or encounter as bloody and pernicious as possible to the first aggressors."[29] Here, moreover, Hume makes no reference to a threat to society's very preservation. It seems, then, that a civilized nation may dispense with justice against an uncivilized enemy even when society's interests, and not its very life, are at stake.

The problem with Hume's argument here is not his suggestion that the rules of just conduct may be different in extreme situations than they are in ordinary ones, or that a threat to self-preservation may modify one's moral obligations. The strictest moralists of the tradition of which John Paul II is a part would admit as much. For that tradition, too, self-preservation is ordinarily not only a legitimate aspiration but even a duty. The crucial difference, however, is this: for Hume, as for Hobbes, self-preservation and even self-interest take on an authority that they cannot possess in the thought of John Paul II. For the pope, recall, the moral law is holy; it is intimately bound up with God as man's supreme and transcendent good. Obedience to it is therefore more important than the safeguarding of any other interest, including one's interest in self-preservation. This is not the case for Hume. For him, justice is not holy but useful, useful with a view to some good other than itself, specifically the satisfaction of our self-interested and sociable desires. Thus when justice no longer serves those ends, it no longer obliges. "By rendering justice totally useless," Hume observes, "you thereby totally destroy its essence, and suspend its obligation upon mankind."[30]

Thus, to return to one of Hume's specific examples, the difficulty in his discussion of war is not his suggestion that in combat with a barbaric opponent harsh measures may be morally justifiable that would not have been so with an enemy who observed the laws of war. Even the most scrupulous adherent of just war theory would likely concede this. It is rather his suggestion that what is justifiable will be determined solely in relation to society's interests. For Hume, it would seem, human life as human life has no intrinsic value. The lives of the members of a nation with whom one is at war have no inherent worth or dignity that commands some minimal respect in all circumstances. Rather, their value is wholly conditioned on their relationship to one's own interests. If showing restraint in war with them procures restraint on their part and thus is advantageous with a view to the security of one's own people, one may posit and observe a certain respect for their lives. But if they show no restraint, one may do likewise. The grievous character of Hume's teaching becomes clear if we consider the implications of his argument, implications that, although left unspoken by Hume, follow of necessity from his principles. One of the most important rules of civilized warfare is that which requires discrimination between enemy combatants and enemy noncombatants. Hume's blanket claims about the basis of the "rules" of war, however, suggests that a nation may abandon even this principle if the other side declines to observe it. If one's enemy stoops to the deliberate killing of innocents to terrorize the civilian population and so erode support for the war, then one may do the same. For Hume, in such circumstances there is no longer any good to be realized through moral restraint, because for him the good resides not in the objective demands of the moral law, or the intrinsic dignity of the human person that the moral law safeguards, but in the satisfaction of nonmoral needs and desires.

Hume, as we have seen, offers a utilitarian understanding of justice. Nevertheless, his emphasis on man's natural sociability and sympathy often leads him to speak of justice in terms of its usefulness *to society*. To this extent he avoids the thoroughgoing individualism of Hobbes, who, we recall, insists that each man consents to the formation of the sovereign, and hence to the institution of justice, with nothing more in view than *his own* self-preservation. As a result, when Hume speaks of the permissibility and reasonableness of rejecting justice when it is no longer useful, we may suspect that he means only that society, not the individual, may dispense with justice when it is necessary to society's survival. This understanding is implied by one of the examples Hume produces in support of his argument. Even when society is not on the point of perishing, he notes, the "*public* . . . opens granaries, without the consent of the proprietors; as justly supposing, that the authority of magistracy may, consistent with equity, extend so far."[31] This, of course, is not yet the natural amorality and anarchy that informs both the culture of death and the political philosophy of Hobbes.

Nevertheless, Hume finally also admits that "necessity and self-preservation" are "stronger motives" than justice for individuals as well as society, and hence that the individual may dispense with justice when his interests so require.[32] This concession follows necessarily from his claim that the self-interested desires are commonly more powerful in human nature than sympathy, which is the source of our commitment to justice. Indeed, this understanding is already present in Hume's afore-mentioned discussion of a society on the brink of starvation. In such extremities, he argues, not only may the authorities responsible for society release themselves from the ordinary obligations of justice in order to preserve society, but "*every man* may now provide for *himself* by *all the means*, which prudence can dictate, or humanity permit."[33] Hume similarly considers the case of a good man who falls "into the society of ruffians, remote from the protection of laws and government." Such a man "must consult the dictates of self-preservation alone" and "make provision of all means of defence and security" regardless of justice, which is "no longer of USE to his own safety or that of others."[34]

Despite his acknowledgement of a natural sociability that is ignored or downplayed in the thought of Hobbes and Locke, Hume finally follows them in making individual self-preservation the fundamental consideration. As we have seen in the case of Locke, however, this elevation of self-preservation tends to open the door to tyranny, at least by undermining the motives to resistance to it when it is inflicted on others. Hume's example of a man fallen into the company of ruffians calls to mind other examples, and raises other questions, beyond those Hume openly addresses. For instance, what if these ruffians are sufficiently disciplined and organized that they do not waste all their strength on pointless violence among themselves but instead seek to despoil and kill others? What if the virtuous man who falls into their company, far from the protection of the law, finds that the only way to preserve himself is to join this band of robbers in their works of injustice? On Hume's principles he must do so. These considerations, however, remind us that in some cases government itself will be no better than a gang of criminals. Such is the language, for example, that Winston Churchill used to describe the Nazi regime. That is, government may sometimes be tyrannical. For the citizen caught in such a regime, Hume's principles point to a policy of nonresistance, and even of active collaboration, if this is necessary for self-preservation. Thus Hume's teachings stand with Locke's in opposition to the argument of John Paul II that the holiness of the moral law prohibits one's cooperation in acts of evil.

The implications of Hume's teaching, however, point even further in this unsavory direction; for his arguments imply that it would be reasonable for a man to embrace injustice not only to avoid the ultimate loss, loss of life itself, but even with a view to selfish gain. Again, it is, on Hume's account, our natural sympathy that interests us in justice, since justice safeguards the well-being of our fellow creatures. Nevertheless, he admits, as we have seen, that the selfish desires are for the most part more powerful than sympathy. Insofar as Hume seeks to derive his morality from the natural sentiments, or insofar as he insists that reason is and should be nothing more than the slave of the passions, violations of justice that advance one's own interests will appear good and reasonable. At this point, of course, the willful pursuit of tyranny has already been embraced in principle. For if the individual's good can be secured by disregard for justice when opportunity presents itself, then individuals united into a tyrannical faction can equally secure their corporate good by abusing the power of government.

This is not to say, of course, that Hume intends such consequences. On the contrary, he openly disclaims them. The argument by which he does so, however, is unpersuasive. As the *Enquiry Concerning the Principles of Morals* draws to a close, Hume turns "briefly to consider our interested *obligation*" to virtue, hoping to show that "every man, who has any regard to his own happiness and welfare," will find these advanced by "the practice of every moral duty." If he can show this on the basis of his theory, Hume notes, he will have the "satisfaction" of having put forward a teaching that "may contribute to the amendment of men's lives, and their improvement in morality and social virtue," rather than one that "leads to a practice dangerous and pernicious." [35] On his theory, Hume argues, virtue is in "the true interest of each individual" because it is naturally enjoyable, responding, as it does, to our natural sociable desires. Hence in making his closing case for virtue he appeals to the pleasures of "benevolence and friendship, humanity and kindness."[36] Of themselves, however, such considerations would not seem a sufficient recommendation for virtue to most human beings, in whom, as Hume has admitted, the desires that look to one's private good are more powerful than those that interest one in the well-being of others. It is perhaps with this difficulty in mind that Hume adds to his defense of virtue a reference to the advantages that accompany a "reputation" for benevolence.[37] To this extent his concluding argument recapitulates the entire *Enquiry*, which repeatedly suggests that virtue is choiceworthy to some extent because of the natural satisfactions that accompany it and to some extent on the basis of self-interested calculation.

The argument thus far, however, does not provide sufficient support for a principled respect for the rights and dignity of other human beings. For we may encounter situations in which a deviation from virtue will advance our interests, the person with whom we are dealing has little hold on our sympathy or benevolence, and we think—like Glaucon in Plato's *Republic*—that our cleverness will allow us to get away with our reputation intact. Hume acknowledges this difficulty. Claiming to treat "vice with the greatest candour, and making it all possible concessions," he holds that it is not preferable to virtue "with a view to self-interest; except, perhaps, in the case of justice, where a man, taking things in a certain light, may often seem to be a loser by his integrity." Thus a "sensible knave" might conclude that he can safely bring off certain injustices without "causing any considerable breach in the social union." In light of these considerations, Hume concedes, one might conclude that "honesty is the best policy" generally, but is also "liable to many exceptions"; and accordingly that he "conducts himself with most wisdom, who observes the general rule, and takes advantage of the exceptions."[38] Here Hume, like Hobbes before him, implicitly confronts the

Machiavellian claim that injustice is good and reasonable when one can get away with it.

As we have seen, Hobbes responds to Machiavelli by suggesting that injustice is unreasonable because there is a good chance that one will *not* get away with it. Hume, too, avails himself of something like this argument, pointing out that we often see "knaves, with all their pretended cunning and abilities, betrayed by their own maxims" and hence suffering a "total loss of reputation, and the forfeiture of all future trust and confidence with mankind."[39] Such arguments, however, by reducing the motive to justice to one of mere self-interest, fail both to provide a solid support for it and to differentiate Hume from Hobbes in the manner that the former seeks. Hume accordingly brings forward a second argument for justice. He notes that while some men will be tempted to profit from injustice when they can, "in all ingenuous natures, the antipathy to treachery and roguery is too strong to be counterbalanced by any view of profit or pecuniary advantage." He continues that "the honest man, if he has any tincture of philosophy, or even of common observation and reflection," will find that knaves are "in the end, the greatest dupes," because they sacrifice "the invaluable enjoyment of a character"—that is, an upright reputation—"with themselves at least, for the acquisition of worthless toys." There is, he adds, no "comparison between the unbought satisfaction of conversation, society, study, even health and the common beauties of nature, but above all the peaceful reflection on one's own conduct," on the one hand, and "the feverish, empty amusements of luxury and expense," on the other.[40] In sum, Hume argues that, on his teaching, injustice is not reasonable because the greatest pleasures cannot be obtained through injustice and are in fact impeded by injustice.

Hume's teaching would appear to fall into incoherence at this point. That is, he can only advance such a defense of justice by abandoning his earlier commitment to establishing his moral philosophy only on what can be gleaned from "experience" or from "fact and observation."[41] Of course, observation and experience cannot of themselves yield a coherent moral theory, because we are bound to observe that different kinds of people behave quite differently. Hume knows this, and he accordingly rejects some observable behavior for the purposes of his moral theory. It is, for example, a matter of "fact and observation" that some people profess and practice what Hume derides as the "monkish virtues." Nevertheless, Hume denies that such virtues deserve a place in his moral teaching, dismissing them as mere products of "superstition."[42] Hume's project then, like that of Hobbes and Locke, is to bring morality down to earth, so to speak, to devise a moral teaching that conforms to human behavior as it is ordinarily observed, or one that is derived from, in Hume's own words, "a cautious observation of human life" as it appears "in the common course of the world," or from the "common and natural course of our passions."[43] It strains credibility, however, to suggest that the ordinary human being will share Hume's sense that the pleasures of luxury are so far inferior to those of sociability, study, and a clear conscience that even successful injustice should be viewed as profitless. After all, as Locke observes, the "greater part" of men are such as to be "no strict observers of equity and justice."[44] Hume, too, implicitly admits as much when he suggests that most men would not respect justice if it were not for the punishments imposed by "positive law" and "government."[45] In the end, then, Hume can only reject successful injustice by means of a tactic inconsistent with his resolution to take his bearings from what is common: he disdains injustice by adopting the perspective of the man of rare refinement of character and mind, that of the "ingenuous" nature, or of the noble and honorable man, and even of the philosopher who derives pleasure from "study."[46] Hobbes was more consistent when he held to "Fear" as the "Passion to be reckoned upon" in securing justice among men who are primarily self-interested, despite noting, but declining to organize his teaching around, a "Generosity too rarely found to be presumed on."[47] Machiavelli surely exaggerated but was nevertheless also more consistent than Hume when he remarked that, for all practical purposes, "in this world there is no one but the vulgar."[48]

THE MORAL LIMITS OF SYMPATHY

In sum, Hume's embrace of a Machivellian and Hobbesian realism dooms his effort to establish a salutary ethical theory, one that will lead men to embrace their moral duties. The combination of his determination to take his bearings from the common and ordinary passions, on the one hand, and his contention that self-interest generally predominates in human nature, on the other, removes the basis for a principled commitment to justice. It thus opens the same individualistic door to outright tyranny that we have found in Hobbes and Locke. Be that as it may, however, it is also true that Hume's teaching would be susceptible to tyranny even if it did not finally embrace a Hobbesian and Lockean individualism. That is, the natural sympathy upon which Hume seeks to establish the human commitment to justice and the social virtues is insufficient to the task even apart from his ultimate subordination of it to individual self-interest.

To begin with, we may observe that sympathy is, on Hume's own account, merely a feeling by which we share in the feelings of others, whatever those feelings may be. Hume's teaching on this matter can be clarified by a reference to the physics of music, in relation to which the term sympathy is also used, and with a meaning similar to Hume's. Strike a key on the piano, and the corresponding wire's vibration will set off sympathetic vibrations in other wires—regardless, of course, whether it was fitting or proper to strike the particular key in question. Similarly, on Hume's account the movements of passion in one human being set off the same movements in others. As a result, sympathy can provide no sure path to justice when we observe a clash of feelings between two of our fellow beings. The difficulty remains even if it is true, as Hume humanely suggests, that sympathy is more easily aroused by another's suffering than another's anger. The anger may be justified, and we may be misled by our sympathy for its object. Besides, in many disputes it will appear to the observer that both parties are suffering in one way or another. In such cases sympathy alone cannot tell us with whom we ought to sympathize.[49]

Moreover, sympathy by its nature tends to make us more partial to some human beings than to others. According to Hume, not only is sympathy "much fainter" than self-concern, but "sympathy with persons remote from us" is "much fainter than that with persons near and contiguous." Consequently, the action of sympathy does not in all cases lend support to justice. Again, Hume himself observes that because of sympathy "the heart" fails to govern "all its love and hatred" according to virtue, "without regard to . . . the persons with whom we are more intimately connected." Similarly, Hume elsewhere notes that not only "self-love" but also "benevolence and humanity" sometimes incline us to "measures of conduct very different from those, which are agreeable to the strict rules of right and justice." Indeed, the operations of sympathy can lead to the most grievous injustices, when human beings, in order to advance the fortunes of those to whom they are united by common interest or kinship, disregard the dignity and rights of others to whom they are not so closely connected. Thus Hume acknowledges "[p]opular sedition, party zeal," and "a devoted obedience to factious leaders" as "some of the most visible, though less laudable effects of this social sympathy in human nature."[50] As a result, the door to tyranny is already opened by Hume's contention, noted earlier, that society may release itself from the obligations of justice in the pursuit of sufficiently compelling interests. Given the emphasis that Hume lays on our natural sympathy, we might be tempted to view this societal dispensation from justice as an act of large scale benevolence: all agreeing to suspend the rules of justice for the sake of all. Given Hume's account of human nature, however, it is much more likely to be a suspension of justice by some faction within society for its own sake and at the expense of other, less favored elements in the society. Put another way, even apart from his concessions to individualistic self-interest, Hume already lays the groundwork for the kind of abuses that concern John Paul II by his claim that in war one society may treat the lives of enemies as if they have no intrinsic value, as if their worth is to be determined only in relation to the society's interests. For, again, this amounts to an admission that human life as human life has no intrinsic value, but that it derives whatever value it has from the self-interested and sociable feelings of whoever is valuing—or not valuing—it. Yet even *within* a society there will be some groups to whom the dominant faction will have no ties of sympathy or interest that could provide a motivation to respect and justice. On the contrary, the ties of sympathy among members of the dominant faction will make them feel justified in their efforts to subordinate the rights and dignity of others to their own group-interest.

In sum, even Hume's emphasis on natural human sympathy is compatible with tyranny. Tyranny, after all, need not be undertaken on the basis of a completely self-interested materialism. The tyrant is often ani-

mated by sociable motives—by his sympathetic concern for some seg-
ment of the society that he aids, at the expense of others, through his
tyrannical rule. In fact, no tyranny could endure unless it had supporters within the society, supporters who justify their cooperation in the
worst injustices by the bonds of sympathy they feel for each other. The
same is true of the contemporary form of tyranny that John Paul II
calls the culture of death. Practices like abortion and euthanasia may
gain credibility as a result of materialistic and individualistic values.
Nevertheless, as *Evangelium Vitae* also suggests, they are commonly chosen on the basis of a misplaced sympathy, a sympathy informed by a preoccupation with materialism and hedonism rather than by an account of
the intrinsic dignity of the human person. Thus do we sometimes seek
to dispose of inconvenient human lives not only out of individual self-
interest but also because of the burdens they impose on others about
whom we care. Indeed, the culture of death, understood as a culture that
publicly justifies such practices, depends on the solidarity, so to speak, of
citizens who sympathize with each others' fear of the demands of caring
for the weak and the accompanying desire to release themselves from
the demands of the moral law when it seems to ask too much.

CONCLUSION

Our earlier discussion of Hobbes indicates that a political teaching organized around individual self-interest inevitably tends to undermine our
regard for human dignity. The case of Hume reveals that human dignity
fares no better under a political teaching organized around individual
self-interest qualified by a natural sociability and sympathy. The moral
consequences of Hume's teaching that justice depends on utility—or on
what seems useful to beings chiefly concerned with the satisfactions of
a hedonistic gregariousness—are revealed with particular clarity in a
single passage of the *Enquiry Concerning the Principles of Morals*:

> Were there a species of creatures, intermingled with men, which,
> though rational, were possessed of such inferior strength, both of body
> and mind, that they were incapable of all resistance, and could never,
> upon the highest provocation, make us feel the effects of their resent-
> ment; the necessary consequence, I think, is, that we should be bound,

by the laws of humanity, to give gentle usage to these creatures, but should not, properly speaking, lie under any restraint of justice with regard to them, nor could they possess any right or property, exclusive of such arbitrary lords. Our intercourse with them could not be called society, which supposes a degree of equality; but absolute command on the one side, and servile obedience on the other. Whatever we covet, they must instantly resign: Our permission is their only tenure, by which they hold their possessions: Our compassion and kindness the only check, by which they curb our lawless will: And as no inconvenience ever results from the exercise of a power, so firmly established in nature, the restraints of justice and property, being totally *useless*, would never have place in so unequal a confederacy.[51]

This passage is striking in the first place because it anticipates, and justifies, the subordination of precisely those vulnerable classes of people with whom John Paul II is concerned in *Evangelium Vitae*. After all, the unborn, the disabled, and those who have suffered catastrophic illness or injury, possess "rational" capacities at least potentially as a result of their sharing in human nature, yet are also so "inferior" in "body and mind" that they cannot resist, or even complain about, ill treatment. On Hume's principles, one cannot speak of justice in relation to such persons. They can have no rights. To be sure, Hume suggests here, as elsewhere, that in the absence of justice simple humanity may still protect the weak.[52] In light of his account of human nature, however, this would seem to be an empty promise. If self-love is more powerful than humanity, there is little real hope that the latter will restrain the former where material interests are at stake. Moreover, we are unlikely to feel much sympathy for such beings, because their inferiority of mind will make it in some cases hard, and in other cases impossible, for them to engage our feelings by effectively expressing their suffering. Indeed, in the immediate sequel to the passage above Hume suggests that in practice serious inequalities of strength will likely obliterate both justice and humanity, and that such inequalities can be found in more than just a handful of human beings. Thus he notes that the "great superiority" of "civilized" Europeans above "barbarous" Indians has "tempted" the former to think themselves fundamentally superior to the latter, and hence to "throw off all restraints of justice, and even of humanity, in our treatment of them."[53] If our regard for others depends not on their intrinsic value as images of God, but on their ability to threaten our interests and command our sympathy, then not only the unborn and disabled, but even weaker peoples of an alien culture, will be subject to unrestrained exploitation. Or, as John Paul II suggests, once we abandon belief in the transcendent dignity of human life as human life, there is no avoiding the culture of death or more obvious forms of tyranny.

Chapter 6

THE AMBIGUITY OF
THE AMERICAN FOUNDING

As we have seen thus far, the arguments of John Paul II's *Evangelium Vitae* imply a critique of various strands of liberal modernity. This is most clear in the case of Hobbes, who forthrightly affirms all the principles and openly draws all the conclusions that the pope associates with the modern erosion of respect for human rights. Hobbes begins from premises that are explicitly individualistic and materialistic, as well as at least implicitly atheistic. As a result, he presents the moral law not as intrinsically good and a path to the highest happiness, but instead as something merely devised by human beings with a view to securing individual self-interest. Yet, as John Paul II contends, and as the argument of *Leviathan* seems to bear out, such a teaching reduces our obligations to each other to a matter of selfish calculation, and therefore can sustain no principled respect for rights and is indeed open to outright tyranny. The cases of Locke and Hume are more complex. Such thinkers are critical of Hobbes but also influenced by him, and their teachings, without being thoroughly Hobbesian, nevertheless contain Hobbesian elements that tend to undermine a solid respect for rights. Locke, as we have seen, offers a decent theistic natural law that is corroded by a somewhat Hobbesian account of human nature. Hume offers a decent affirmation of a natural human sociability and sympathy that is undercut by his exclusion of the transcendent from his account and by his willingness to concede that self-interest is the core of human nature.

These approaches, however, do not exhaust all of the manifestations of liberal modernity, which may reveal itself in other forms more compatible with *Evangelium Vitae*'s argument. Hobbes, Locke, and Hume are political philosophers of the first rank who, despite their differences, seem united in their characteristically modern determination to make a break with the Aristotelian-Thomistic tradition on which John Paul II draws, especially its understanding of morality as looking ultimately to the supreme good, rather than to the satisfaction of the most commonly powerful human passions. It is this theoretical break that John Paul II finds so radically problematic. While a clean break with the thought of the past may be possible for theorists, however, it is perhaps not so easily effected—indeed may not even be desired—by practitioners, that is, by citizens and statesmen. Thus, if the various political philosophers of liberal modernity are at odds with the teaching of John Paul II, it may nevertheless be that the philosophically informed founders of modern liberal political societies offer a teaching that is more in harmony with the pope's understanding. In particular, we are drawn to the American Founding, with its nods to modern, classical, and Christian principles, as a version of liberal modernity that may avoid the dangers diagnosed by the pope. We turn then to consider the most publicly authoritative presentation of the Founders' understanding of natural law and natural rights, the *Declaration of Independence*.

THE TEACHING OF THE DECLARATION

One can hardly claim to find anything in the *Declaration of Independence* that would be problematic on John Paul II's understanding, and one certainly does find much that he would welcome. The *Declaration* famously begins with an unequivocal assertion of the rights of man: "We hold these truths to be self-evident, that all men are created equal, that they are endowed by their Creator with certain unalienable Rights, that among these are Life, Liberty, and the pursuit of Happiness."[1] This may be taken as a statement of the core of the Founding generation's political morality, and it would seem to achieve the moral objectivity that John Paul II claims is necessary to the preservation of respect for human dignity. Recall that the pope criticizes moral relativism for making respect for fundamental rights seem not absolutely but only conditionally obligatory. Rights, the *Declaration* instructs us, belong to "all men" by virtue of their creation as men. That is, rights are a fact of human nature, or, to use language more reminiscent of John Paul II, rights are inherent in the human person. This is the *Declaration*'s clear meaning, the contentions of later American revisionists to the contrary notwithstanding.[2]

Moreover, on the *Declaration*'s account, as on John Paul II's, the rights of human beings are rooted not only in human nature, but also in a larger natural order. They are, in fact, rooted ultimately in God himself. Thus the *Declaration* speaks of man's rights as having been endowed by man's "Creator," following on earlier language that situated the *Declaration*'s moral argument in the context of the "Law of Nature and of Nature's God." We may say, then, that for both the *Declaration of Independence* and John Paul II, the rights of human beings have a transcendent basis. They are rooted in the cosmic order itself and in its highest principle, and they therefore are derived from an authority that no human power can gainsay. Hence they are "unalienable." Rights cannot justly be separated from their human possessors, either by the violence of other human beings or by the misguided consent of the possessors themselves.

Unalienable because rooted in Nature and Nature's God, the rights of human beings are also binding upon the highest human authorities, that is, upon governments themselves. Indeed, the *Declaration* presents the security of rights as the very end of government, the purpose for which political authority is instituted. And, in light of the moral standard provided by this theory of rights, the *Declaration* can, unlike Hobbes, name tyranny as a morally real phenomenon that calls for rebuke, resistance, and even, in the most extreme cases, rebellion. All this, again, is broadly compatible with John Paul II's argument in *Evangelium Vitae*, which holds, as we have seen, that fundamental human rights are the foundation of the political community and that laws in violation of those rights can be deemed unjust and even tyrannical.

Finally, the moral and political truths of the *Declaration* are held to be "self-evident." That is, they are not aspects of a revelation that has been given to some men only, or elements of a cultural tradition inherited only by a particular people. Rights are rather aspects of a moral law that can be known through the activity of reason and are accordingly accessible, in principle, to human beings everywhere. Hence the willingness of the *Declaration's* authors to lay its argument before a "candid world." John Paul II, it would seem, could scarcely ask for a more secure theoretical foundation for the rights of man.

There is, then, nothing in the *Declaration of Independence* to which John Paul II would likely object. But does it contain everything that he thinks essential? The *Declaration*, after all, may err not by commission but by omission, from the standpoint of *Evangelium Vitae's* account of the basis of human rights and dignity. Considering the *Declaration's* core teaching in light of the previously studied authors, we might say that it is a statement of Lockean political theology—the doctrine that rights are given by God—without the corrosive Hobbesian anthropology that appears in the *Second Treatise*. From John Paul II's standpoint such a teaching is of course preferable to the ambiguities of the *Second Treatise*, to say nothing of the teaching of Hobbes himself. Nevertheless, the theology of *Evangelium Vitae* is a good deal richer than that of the *Second Treatise* or the *Declaration*, and John Paul II presents that theology as necessary to a properly grounded respect for the dignity of human beings. For that matter, John Paul II's account suggests that we need not only a correct theology but also an adequate anthropology, a proper account of man's nature in relation to God's nature, if rights are to be securely founded. Beyond its assertion that human beings have rights, however, the *Declaration* contains no anthropology to speak of.

To clarify these issues, it is necessary to return briefly to the argument of *Evangelium Vitae*. There John Paul II contends that human life cannot be properly valued and protected unless it is understood to have a significance that transcends mere biological existence. It must be understood in relation to life in the highest sense, that is, to the life of God. Human dignity, and the rights that are inseparable from it, are rooted in man's creation in God's "image" and "likeness." Man shares in God's nature. He possesses God-like powers of reason and freedom. He is therefore due a respect commensurate with his lofty status. The *Declaration*, in contrast, offers no such understanding. It presents man as possessing rights from God, but not as being God-like. On the

Declaration's account—and, for that matter, on the account of Section 6 of Locke's *Second Treatise*—God creates man and places on him a kind of "Private Property: No Trespassing" sign. For John Paul II, man is himself a sign of the transcendent dignity of God, and therefore shares in that dignity.

John Paul II also emphasizes the loftiness of the human vocation as a basis of man's inviolable dignity. For him, the idea of man as the image of God not only looks back to the nature with which man was endowed, but also looks forward to the realization of his destiny. For human beings are called to perfect the image of God in themselves through actions in accord with the moral law and, ultimately, through loving service of their fellows. This, the pope teaches, is the path to union with God, the supreme good and final end for man, and therefore to the achievement of the highest and most genuine human happiness. This understanding, he suggests, renders the rights of all secure, because by it we transcend the conflicts of material interest that tempt us to violate each other's rights. We are led to respect the dignity of others because we realize that we win our own happiness precisely in actions that manifest that respect. Once again, the *Declaration* is silent on these issues. It says nothing about man's final end. It speaks of man's rights, but it does not explain their relationship to man's purpose. To be sure, there is at least a gesture toward man's end in the reference to the "pursuit of Happiness." Man has a right to seek his end. The *Declaration*, however, leaves us in doubt as to the precise character of human happiness, and in particular its relationship to the "Laws of Nature and of Nature's God." Is each man's happiness to be found in works that actualize a respect for the moral law and for other human beings? Or is that happiness to be found in other, unspecified works, the possibility of which is protected by the laws of nature and nature's God, but the activity of which is otherwise unrelated to those laws? The *Declaration* leaves us in suspense.

On John Paul II's argument, the *Declaration's* omissions are significant because the uncertainties they create are perilous. Without an appreciation of the intrinsic link between the performance of man's duties and the realization of his happiness, he is apt to regard the moral law as, to use a term from *Veritatis Splendor*, a "heteronomy," as an extrinsic imposition on his being that is alien and even hostile to his deepest aspirations. This understanding, the pope reminds us, fosters temptations to evade the requirements of the moral law and hence to disregard the rights of others.

One might respond that the *Declaration* at least hints at an understanding of human life that transcends mere biological existence. After all, the signers of the *Declaration* pledge in support of the revolutionary cause their "Lives," "Fortunes," and "sacred Honor."[3] Does not this promise necessarily imply that there are human goods—goods perhaps identified by the "Laws of Nature and of Nature's God"—that transcend material ease and security, moral goods in the service of which we must be prepared to sacrifice life and wealth? Does it not call to mind even the pope's own claim in *Veritatis Splendor* that the moral law is holy and therefore to be obeyed at any hazard, even the risk of martyrdom?

Certainly the *Declaration* culminates in an elevated sentiment powerfully expressed, yet it is not clear that it carries the import suggested in the preceding remarks. After all, the *Declaration*'s concluding pledge may amount to no more than the enlightened self-interest captured in Ben Franklin's famous remark, "we must, indeed, all hang together, or most assuredly we shall all hang separately."[4] In such a situation, loyalty to the cause is inseparable from self-preservation. The *Declaration*, however, can be read as presenting just such a situation. It suggests that the colonists are compelled to make a revolution because they are confronted with a "design to reduce them under absolute Despotism" or "Tyranny."[5] Thus they are willing to risk all their worldly goods because those goods are already in grave danger, a danger that will only grow with inaction. Of course, such spiritedness in the defense of one's own rights is far more admirable than a paralyzing cowardice that submits to slavery. Yet it is not the same as the love of which John Paul II speaks, the love of the moral law and of the human person that ensures a respect for the rights of others.

In response to the foregoing argument, one might contend that, if the *Declaration*'s anthropology provides an insufficient motive for a principled respect for rights, its theology, considered in full, supplies the deficiency. After all, the *Declaration* presents God not only as the original author, but also the ongoing vindicator, of man's rights. The document opens by invoking God as man's creator, but it concludes by appealing to God as man's "Supreme Judge" and providential protector.[6] Of course, the *Declaration* is overwhelmingly a complaint about injustices perpetrated against those making the declaration, and hardly at all a recognition of their duty to observe justice in their relations with others. Nevertheless, once rational beings invoke God's judgment and providence in defense of their own rights—and especially when they present their argument in terms that can be laid before a presumably disinterested "candid world"—they cannot help but see that these divine forces might be turned against them if they violate the rights of others. Jefferson, the principal drafter of the *Declaration*, later gave eloquent voice to this insight in his *Notes on the State of Virginia*, where he said, in relation to American slavery: "I tremble for my country when I reflect that God is just," because the liberties of men are "the gift of God" and "are not to be violated but with his wrath."[7] Surely, one might conclude, the *Declaration* provides ample incentive to respect the rights of all by implying that their protection is a concern of God's inescapable government of the world.

We suspect nevertheless that John Paul II would find this argument insufficient. This suspicion is provoked, first of all, by his apparent unwillingness to employ such an argument himself. A grim warning about the divine wrath awaiting those who violate human dignity—a kind of fire and brimstone approach—was certainly available to John Paul II, yet he chose not to employ it, emphasizing instead the violence that a person does to his own nature when he commits injustice and the happiness he achieves when he does right. The inadequacy of a mere invocation of divine judgment—in the absence of a fully developed anthropology such as John Paul II offers—is implied, again, by his aforementioned notion of heteronomy. To support justice with *only* an appeal to the possibility of divine punishment is to imply that injustice would be good for its perpetrator were it not for the threatened retribution, were it not for consequences that are imposed artificially and from the outside by a superior power. This in turn implies, however, that justice is not intrinsically choiceworthy, that it is, in the words of *Veritatis Splendor*, merely an imposition of rules of conduct "extraneous to man" and "unrelated to his good."[8] On this view, the just life is nothing more than a form of "alienation," an understanding that is inseparable from a desire to escape the requirements of justice if possible, and that therefore does not provide an adequate motive for men to be just. After all, if men are told that injustice would be in their interest were it not for God's punishments, they will begin to wonder how his punishments might be evaded, a question that will come to mind all the more readily when they believe that God is not only just but also forgiving.

Such deficiencies in an account of justice that supports it with only an appeal to divine punishments was recognized and laid bare at the dawn of political philosophy. In Plato's *Republic*, the author's young brothers, Glaucon and Adeimantus, ask Socrates to demonstrate to them that justice is good for the soul of the just man, apart from any consequences beyond itself. Glaucon asks that justice be praised without reference to the reputation for justice one might earn among fellow citizens, and Adeimantus, upping the ante, asks that it be praised irrespective of the reputation one might win with the gods themselves. As Glaucon notes, praising justice in light of the benefits that come from a just reputation is not truly praise of justice itself, since the clever and spirited can cultivate a just reputation while secretly getting away with injustice. Similarly, Adeimantus contends that those who "extol justice" in light of divine rewards and punishments yet "have nothing else to say" do not offer an adequate defense of just conduct. To those who note that it is impossible to escape the judgments of the gods, he argues that "if there are gods and they care" about justice, then the same sources that inform us of their existence also hold that their justice is not unrelenting. Rather, "they are such as to be persuaded and perverted by sacrifices, soothing vows, and votive offerings." But if this is the case, then "injustice must be done and sacrifice offered for the unjust acquisitions." For if we adhere to justice, we merely go unpunished. "But if we are unjust, we shall gain and get off unpunished as well, by persuading the gods with prayers when we transgress and make mistakes."[9]

The *Declaration of Independence* provides the classic statement of America's moral-political creed. That statement, however, falls short of what John Paul II thinks is necessary to support a reliable respect for the dignity and rights of human beings. Its failings, it would seem, are of omission rather than commission. The *Declaration* articulates an essential truth when it presents the rights of human beings as part of a natural moral order rooted ultimately in God the creator. Nevertheless, its failure to relate that moral order to humanity's final end and highest happiness leaves open the question whether respect for rights is good not only when it protects us from others but also when it obligates us to others. And for John Paul II this omission opens a door to injustice.

BEYOND THE *DECLARATION*

One might defend the American founding from such criticisms by noting that the Declaration's theoretical scope was necessarily limited by its practical purpose. Perhaps it is unreasonable to expect a complete account of the anthropology, theology, and morality that is required for a decent society from what is, after all, a state paper and, in fact, a foreign policy pronouncement. We get an artificially constrained view of the Founders' moral and political theory if we examine only the *Declaration*, because they surely did not intend to say everything they believed in the *Declaration*. We often take the *Declaration* as a complete statement of America's deepest founding principles, but this is not necessarily how it was intended. It may be, then, that the *Declaration*'s shortcomings cannot justly be imputed to the thought of the Founders. For that thought, fleshed out in detail in voluminous writings, might be found to manifest an understanding of morality, human nature, and human happiness similar to that of John Paul II himself. According to this argument, if we look beyond the *Declaration* and sift the thought of the founding generation we may find the essential principles unmentioned or unelaborated in the *Declaration*.

In truth, when we look beyond the *Declaration* we are confronted with a body of political and moral reflection that is ambiguous in its relationship to both the philosophical tradition on which John Paul II draws and the modern theoretical movements to which we have juxtaposed his thought. That is, while there is much in the Founders' discourse that is clearly akin to the arguments of *Evangelium Vitae*, there is also much that is clearly akin to the problematic elements of Hobbes and Locke, which, as we have seen, appear to prefigure the contemporary currents of thought of which the pope is so critical. Let us be clear. This ambiguity exists *not* in relation to the immediate, practical issues which John Paul II takes as the point of departure for his argument. Thus, for example, James Wilson obviously speaks not only for himself but for the whole founding generation when he notes the "consistency, beautiful and undeviating," with which the "common law" protects "human life, from its commencement to its close." In this context he contrasts, in terms that resonate with John Paul II's later concerns, the laudable "anxiety, with which some legal systems spare and preserve human life," on the one hand, with, on the other, the "levity and cruelty which others discover in destroying or sporting with it," as well as "the inconsistency, with which, in others, it is, at some times, wantonly sacrificed, and, at other times, religiously guarded." He singles out for particular condemnation ancient Greece, Rome, and China for the "unnatural practice" of infanticide, which he regards as an example of "barbarity."[10]

Nor does the ambiguity arise with regard to what John Paul II presents as the ultimate consequence of the philosophic errors that he addresses: an openness to rule that is substantively tyrannical although procedurally democratic. For the Founders, of all people, took great pains to make clear their belief that democratic forms are no guarantee against tyranny and that no human power, not even a political majority, possesses a just authority to violate the fundamental rights of human beings. James Madison expressed not just his own conviction but the sense of the great body of the Founding generation when he wrote to James Monroe that the "interest of the majority" cannot be taken simply as the "political standard of right and wrong." "Taking the word 'interest' as synonymous with 'ultimate happiness,' in which sense it is qualified with every necessary moral ingredient, the proposition is no doubt true," Madison concedes. Nevertheless, he continues, taking the term "interest" in the "popular sense, as referring to immediate augmentation" of material wealth, "nothing can be more false" than to equate majority interest with justice. For in this "latter sense it would be the interest of the majority in every community to despoil and enslave the minority of individuals." Such an understanding of democracy Madison concludes—again, in terms reminiscent of *Evangelium Vitae*—simply reestablishes, "under another name and a more specious form, force as the measure of right."[11]

Rather, viewed in light of *Evangelium Vitae*'s argument, the thought of the Founders is ambiguous in regard to the relationship of the moral law to human nature and the supreme good—that is, in relation to the moral-anthropological-theological question on which the *Declaration of Independence* is problematically silent, the crucial theoretical gap we had hoped to fill precisely by looking to founding thought beyond the *Declaration*. Is the moral law a path of self-perfection or merely of self-protection? The discourse of the founding generation points to no clear answer to this vital question.

This ambiguity is reflected in a single statement by one of the leading founders, a remark by the *Declaration*'s principal author intended to explain the document's intellectual underpinnings. Writing to Henry Lee, Thomas Jefferson holds that the *Declaration*'s aim was to "place before mankind the common sense" of the revolutionary position as it appeared to the "American mind." This American understanding, he adds, was informed by "the elementary books of public right, as Aristotle, Cicero, Locke, Sidney, &c."[12] This remark, however, looks simultaneously in two different directions. The reference to Aristotle and Cicero seems to place the founding generation within the same Aristotelian-Thomistic tradition upon which John Paul II relies, a philosophic approach holding that the supreme good for man is realized through the activity of virtue. At the same time, the reference to Locke would appear to place the Founders in a distinctively modern theoretical camp that had come to view virtue as merely the means to peaceable and prosperous living together in society. To be sure, Jefferson was, although admittedly brilliant, a notoriously paradoxical thinker. Nevertheless, we cannot chalk up the tension revealed in this comment to the peculiarities of his own intellect. For the same ambiguity can be perceived generally in the thought of the leading figures of the founding generation.

Some founding political thought is clearly influenced, indirectly at least, by the same intellectual tradition to which John Paul II belongs. For example, the revolutionary writings of a young Alexander Hamilton contain a forthright rejection of the modern understanding of morality as purely instrumental. Hamilton takes issue with the view of "Mr. Hobbs" that man is by nature "free from all restraint of law and government." On this understanding, Hamilton points out, "[m]oral obligation . . . is derived from the introduction of civil society; and there is no virtue, but what is purely artificial, the mere contrivance of politicians, for the maintenance of social intercourse." In contrast to this view, which he takes to be implicitly atheistic, Hamilton holds that God has "constituted an eternal and immutable law, which is, indispensable, obligatory upon all mankind, prior to any human institution whatever."[13] Moreover, John Adams contends that the rights of human beings are linked to the special "dignity" of man's "nature," to the "noble rank he holds among the works of God." Thus "slavery," for example, is not only contrary to the interests of the one enslaved but also "a sacrilegious breach of trust" that is "offensive in the sight of God."[14] Elsewhere, Adams suggests that this "dignity" of man, as well as "his happiness," "consists in virtue."[15] George Washington's 1783 *Circular to the States* concludes by calling upon his countrymen to conduct themselves with "that Charity, humility, and pacific temper of mind, which were the Characteristicks of the Divine Author of our blessed Religion, and without an humble imitation of whose example in these things, we can never hope to be a happy Nation."[16] All of these remarks echo key points of John Paul II's social thought as it is expressed in *Evangelium Vitae.*

If we look beyond the public pronouncements of the leading political figures, we find a body of religious thought—expressed for the most part in political sermons—that articulates even more explicitly the same themes as John Paul II. Exemplary in this regard is Elizur Goodrich's election sermon of May 10, 1787, preached to the governor and legislature of Connecticut. The "principles of society," Goodrich contends, are not, as Hobbes would have it, mere conventions agreed upon by human beings but the "fixed and unchangeable" laws of the "moral world" which "Almighty God has established" to govern men "in their transactions and intercourse" with each other. Moreover, these moral laws are not to be observed primarily with a view to attaining some submoral end, like bodily security, but are themselves the path to the fulfillment of man's true purpose, for they "direct mankind to the highest perfection, and supreme happiness of their nature." In addition, God's law finds its culmination in the gospel, which "does everything for our happiness in this world" that "can be effected by the most excellent precepts of morality," and indeed in the "great and most universal principle and law of rational union and happiness," the "love of God and of our neighbour."[17] In view of such remarks, it would seem that the anthropology and theology that

John Paul II thinks essential to the civilization of rights can be found in the thought of the American founding.

At the same time, however, the thought of the Founders sometimes bespeaks a kind of materialistic individualism which reflects the influence of modern political thought and which John Paul II thinks corrosive of a society's respect for human rights and human dignity. Evidence of such influence is not isolated, but can be found in the arguments of such diverse figures as John Adams and Thomas Jefferson, who seem to represent different philosophic wings of the revolutionary generation. For example, Adams's *Thoughts on Government* suggests that human "happiness" is to be understood as "ease, comfort," and "security"—a formulation that owes much more to Hobbes and Locke than to the Thomistic-Aristotelian tradition on which the pope draws.[18] Such thinking also influences important public documents, such as Adams's draft of the Massachusetts Constitution, the preamble of which tends to reduce the "blessings of life" to "safety, happiness, and prosperity."[19]

Similar tendencies are evident, for example, in Jefferson's "Opinion on the French Treaties," which he wrote in 1793 at President Washington's request in order to elucidate the question whether the United States should renounce its treaties with France. The general direction of Jefferson's argument—which seeks to vindicate America's duty to France by refuting Hamilton's contention that agreements may be unilaterally abandoned when they prove "dangerous, useless, or disagreeable"—implies that moral obligations cannot be based merely on calculations of self-interest.[20] Nevertheless, even when writing with such an aim, Jefferson cannot escape the language and even the conclusions of a Hobbesian modernity. Thus he says that man is subject to a "Moral law" known though "Conscience," but at the same time he reduces conscience, or knowledge of moral principles, to "feelings." Such a view, as we have seen, tends inevitably to equate one's obligations with whatever one most powerfully desires, an understanding that is not conducive to a principled respect for others. As a result, Jefferson is compelled to admit that, in at least a certain extreme case, the laws of morality must be subordinated to individual self-interest. Thus he concedes that an agreement may be abandoned when performance is "self-destructive to the party," for "the law of self-preservation overrules the laws of obligation to others."[21] One might defend Jefferson on the grounds that probably everybody would agree that a nation is exempted from its treaty agreements when they are destructive of the nation itself. Be that as it may, however, Jefferson here presents his argument in terms that are equally applicable to nations and individuals—indeed, he suggests that the moral law is the same for both. Thus his argument embraces the Lockean assumption that self-preservation is the supreme and most sacred law of nature, in contrast to the pope's view that the moral law is holy and sometimes may demand martyrdom. As we have seen in the case of Locke, however, once the moral law is so understood, it is difficult to maintain a morality that is distinct from self-interest. Given the power of our self-regard, we tend to identify our self-preservation with whatever can be plausibly connected to it, and ultimately with whatever we want, with the result that moral obligations are more and more subordinated to considerations of self-interest. The first stages of this moral unraveling are evident even in Jefferson's "Opinion," which first holds that we need not perform obligations when they are "self-destructive," but soon moves on to exempt us from them when they merely present a "danger." To be sure, Jefferson, seeking to distinguish his position from Hamilton's, insists that this danger be "great, inevitable & imminent." But a mind preoccupied with self-preservation as the fundamental good will tend to inflate the greatness of any threat, and will surely ask why it must tolerate threats that are not imminent when they are inevitable.

I do not, of course, intend the previous discussion as anything like a comprehensive account of founding political thought beyond the *Declaration of Independence*. Such an account is outside the scope of the present chapter and the present book. The passages on which I have relied, however, do illustrate, to the extent that this study requires, the moral and philosophic diversity of founding thought, a diversity from which arises its ambiguous relationship to the thought of John Paul II. Indeed, this diversity is deep enough that even those who undertake comprehensive studies of the political theory of the founding cannot agree on the predominant intellectual tradition shaping it, or even whether it can be understood in terms of a single predominant tradition.[22]

CONCLUSION

From the standpoint of John Paul II's argument in *Evangelium Vitae*, the political theory of the American Founding must be viewed with a certain ambivalence. On the one hand, the *Declaration of Independence* offers a decent account of the rights of human beings as rooted in a transcendent moral order, and even in the will of God himself. To this extent our most important founding document seems to render America proof against the erosion of respect for rights that the pope sees in the modern world. On the other hand, the *Declaration* seems to offer only an incomplete anthropology, morality, and theology. It remains silent on the question of the relationship of morality to man's truest happiness and his quest for the supreme good, and to that extent lacks elements that the pope believes are essential to maintaining a solid respect for the rights and dignity of all human beings. Looking beyond the *Declaration* to the broader political discourse of the founding generation, we find an emphasis on the importance of Christian love more or less the same as that articulated by John Paul II himself. Then again, that discourse also reveals powerful strains of thought emphasizing an individualism that in some cases verges on the Hobbesian. Overall, the political theory of the American founding would seem to have some elements that the pope would consider cause for alarm, but also other, more wholesome elements to which one could fruitfully appeal in defense of a principled respect for the rights of all. Indeed, John Paul II did not hesitate to invoke such elements for such purposes when the opportunity presented itself.[23]

Nevertheless, it would seem that over time the wholesome elements in the founding have tended to lose their power over the American mind, which has tended increasingly to embrace the kind of Hobbesian individualism and hedonism that make the moral law appear a burden and respect for the rights of others a matter of mere self-interested calculation. Put more bluntly, America has shown itself susceptible to the moral and intellectual currents characterized by the pope as the "culture of death." This, at least, appears to be John Paul II's own diagnosis. There is, after all, no obvious reason to exclude contemporary America from the pope's criticisms, noted in chapter 2, of the nations of the developed west. On the contrary, his 1999 Apostolic Exhortation, *Ecclesia in America,* appears explicitly to apply such criticisms to America.[24]

We are led, then, to wonder why America has developed in such a manner. Why has a materialistic individualism tended to prevail? Conversely, why have the more generous elements in the thought of the American founding failed to prevent the crisis of respect for rights that the pope now observes? To answer these questions, I propose that we turn to Alexis de Tocqueville's account of how democratic social conditions influence the thoughts and sentiments of modern man.

Chapter 7

TOCQUEVILLE AND THE MORAL TRAJECTORY OF MODERN DEMOCRACY

At first glance, one might expect modern democracy as Tocqueville presents it to be broadly congenial to John Paul II's call for a "civilization of love." Modern democracy, after all, is founded upon equality. In America, Tocqueville claims, equality is the "generative fact" from which almost everything flows. Generally, democratic peoples love equality above everything else, even freedom itself.[1] On Tocqueville's account, however, the modern rise of equality finds its ultimate origins in Christianity. In his "Introduction" to *Democracy in America*, he credits the Church with introducing equality into European society, and he suggests that the modern movement toward democracy is coextensive with "the Christian universe."[2] Indeed, Tocqueville at least comes close to suggesting that the very idea of human equality, and hence of the rights and dignity of human beings as human beings, could never have been introduced absent the Christian revelation. The ancient world, he notes, was dominated by an aristocratic social state that naturally led the mind to view men not in terms of their humanity but their class or rank. "The most profound and vast geniuses of Rome and Greece," he contends, "were never able to arrive at the idea, so general but at the same time so simple, of the similarity of men and of the equal right to freedom that each bears from birth." Their intellects were "limited" by the "aristocracy of masters" that was "established without dispute before their eyes," and it was accordingly "necessary that Jesus Christ come to earth to make it understood that all members of the human species are naturally alike and equal."[3]

Nevertheless, whatever the merits of the Christian conception of equality—that all men, as created in the image and likeness of God, possess an inherent dignity that should command the respect of their fellows—Tocqueville also indicates that the rise of modern, democratic equality is far from unproblematic. The aim of Tocqueville's book is to identify and recommend the cultural and political institutions by which this equality can be made compatible with "freedom," "enlightenment," and "prosperity." To this extent his argument is inseparable from a hope for the best. In politics as in medicine, however, while prescription must imply hope, diagnosis may still give rise to dread. This is certainly the case for Tocqueville, whose argument indicates that democracy's unchecked propensities can lead to "servitude," "barbarism," and "misery."[4] Indeed, Tocqueville's account suggests that modern democracy fosters precisely those habits of thought that John Paul II presents as eroding contemporary society's ability to maintain a principled respect for the rights and dignity of all.

DEMOCRACY AND THE ECLIPSE OF GOD

John Paul II contends, as we have seen, that the deepest root of the negation of human dignity is the loss of a sense of God. On his account, the rights of human beings are adequately safeguarded only when the moral law is understood to be rooted in God as the supreme good. Only then can morality be accepted as objectively true and inherently good, and hence as both binding on and good for everyone, even those upon whom it may impose an obligation to sacrifice their material interests in the service of others. In the absence of God, on the other hand, men come to view the moral law as something relatively, rather than absolutely, good—a merely human contrivance devised with a view to merely human interests. Thus even fundamental rights become negotiable and the weak vulnerable to exploitation or even extermination.

Tocqueville's thought points to similar conclusions. Religious belief, he argues, is necessary to any society as the basis of the minimal level of common thought and common action that social living requires. Tocqueville contends that all human actions, no matter how small, proceed from some "general idea that men have conceived of God, of his relations with the human race, of the nature of their souls, and of their duties to those like them." Accordingly, men have an "immense interest" in establishing "very fixed ideas for themselves" on these matters, because "doubt about these first points would deliver all their actions to chance and condemn them to a sort of disorder and impotence." Tocqueville's remark that "doubt" about religious questions leads to "disorder," to human actions being guided by "chance," would seem to imply something like John Paul II's view that belief in God is needed to sustain a principled respect for morality. This similarity is rendered more clear in the sequel. For Tocqueville proceeds to argue that when "religion is destroyed in a people, doubt takes hold of the highest portions of the intellect and half paralyzes all the others." Men are then reduced to having "only confused and changing notions about" the most important questions, and a "limitless independence" opens up before them.[5] Elsewhere, Tocqueville speaks even more openly of "religion" as having provided men with the "most visible boundary" between "good and evil," in the absence of which all has come to appear "doubtful and uncertain in the moral world."[6]

Tocqueville also indicates, however, that modern democracy tends to undermine man's sense of God, thus eroding the most solid basis for morality. Democratic men, he contends, "are naturally little disposed to believe" as a result of the influence of the social state upon their minds.[7] Democrats, it seems, are natural Cartesians. Thus Tocqueville's Americans do not read Descartes because their "social state turns them away from speculative studies," yet "they follow his maxims because this same social state naturally disposes their minds to adopt them." These maxims, according to Tocqueville, are rationalistic: democrats tend to "seek the reason for things by themselves and in themselves alone," each man relying "only on the individual effort of his reason." Such a philosophic method is insinuated into the mind by the equality of conditions characteristic of a democratic social state. Deference to intellectual authority comes easy to the people of an aristocracy, for the severe inequalities of the social state—and of its educational opportunities, which are extensive and refined for the few, and more or less nonexistent for the many—make them accustomed to seeing "incontestable signs of greatness and superiority" in some men. In a democracy, by contrast, all men have some access to education, are therefore roughly equal in their intellectual attainments, and accordingly "are constantly led back toward their own reason as the most visible and closest source of truth." This rationalism, however, in turn diminishes the democratic man's receptivity to the supernatural. Precisely because they succeed in conducting their personal affairs independently and on the basis of their own reason, Tocqueville suggests, democratic men come to "conclude that everything in the world is explicable and that nothing exceeds the bounds of intelligence." They accordingly "deny what they cannot comprehend" and develop "an almost invincible distaste for the supernatural."[8]

Moreover, democracy, according to Tocqueville's argument, not only erodes the credibility of belief in God, it also leads to a forgetfulness of the very idea of God. Language, Tocqueville notes, is "the first instrument of thought." The social state, however, exerts a powerful influence on language, and hence tends to shape the kind of thoughts that may be easily entertained. In an aristocracy, for example, society is ruled by a class of men freed, from birth to death, from necessary work, and accordingly enjoying leisure for the works of the mind. The language in such a society will naturally take on an elevated tone. In a democracy, on the other hand, society is ruled by the majority or "the people"—by men equal and independent, none of whom enjoys a leisured status secured by law, and most of whom therefore need to work in order to live. The language in such a society will lean toward the worldly and practical. In a democracy, Tocqueville observes, "the majority make the law in the matter of language just as in everything else." Since they are concerned primarily with business, commerce, and party politics, their words will "serve mainly to express" these needs. "The language will constantly stretch in that direction, whereas on the contrary it will abandon little by little the terrain of metaphysics and theology."[9]

Finally, Tocqueville suggests that whatever concept of God can be retained in democracy will tend to be one of diminished grandeur, for equality of conditions fosters pantheism. Democrats, it seems, have a passion for "general ideas," a desire to link all phenomena as much as possible to a single cause. This mental propensity, again, reflects the influence of the social state. Aristocrats have an aversion to general ideas, because the society they inhabit continually imposes notions of particularity upon their minds. The inhabitants of an aristocracy find themselves surrounded by men of different rank and status, and are therefore accustomed to think of human affairs in terms of fundamental differences among men. They ultimately carry such habits of thought into their reflection on all things. Conversely, the inhabitants of a democracy, finding society made up of "beings who are almost the same," spontaneously think in terms of humanity itself, rather than in terms of the various kinds of men. Again, this habit of thought influences all of their thinking on every subject, and "thus the need to discover common rules for all things, to enclose many objects within the same form, and to explain a collection of facts by a single cause becomes an ardent and often blind passion of the human mind."[10]

This democratic taste for general ideas, however, fosters pantheism. The "idea of unity obsesses" the democratic mind, and at first this may lead to an inclination to monotheism: democrats are easily led to the notion of a single creation and a single creator. Nevertheless, so powerful is the democratic mind's craving for intellectual unity that even the distinction between creation and creator "still bothers it, and it willingly seeks to enlarge and simplify its thought by enclosing God and the universe within a single whole." Such a system—for which "all things material and immaterial, visible and invisible, that the world includes" will be "no more than diverse parts of an immense being"—will hold "secret charms for men who live in democracy."[11]

On Tocqueville's view, moreover, pantheism threatens to degrade the human spirit. Hence his call for "all who remain enamored of the genuine greatness of man" to "unite and do combat against it."[12] Tocqueville does not explain how pantheism imperils human greatness, but we might surmise that something like the following argument informs his judgment. The idea of "greatness"—if it is to refer to something besides mere size, as indeed Tocqueville seems to intend here—necessarily implies some hierarchy of being and of values according to which we can judge some thoughts, sentiments, actions, and characters as more elevated than others. Pantheism, however, forbids any such hierarchy. By equating God with the world, it divinizes everything—the noble and the base, the beautiful and the ugly, the selfless and the selfish. Rather, it obliterates any fundamental qualitative distinction between these things by identifying them all equally with the divine. This in turn destroys any reason to strive for one thing more than another. Put simply, genuine greatness seems to have no meaning in the absence of the transcendent, yet pantheism destroys our sense of the transcendent.

Here we may return for a moment to John Paul II, for it would seem that on Tocqueville's account democracy obscures the understanding of God that the pope thinks necessary to sustaining our respect for the dignity of human life. For the Holy Father, recall, human life is not properly understood or valued except in relation to life in the highest sense—the divine life of God. Every human being is owed some respect—even, we might say, some veneration—because every human being is created in the image and likeness of a transcendent God. Moreover, we can speak of the dignity of human life in relation to the loftiness of the human vocation—to perfect our likeness to God through the fulfillment of our vocation to love and serve others according to God's law. Pantheism, however, renders such notions unintelligible. For if God is the universe, then every being, and every way of being, are equally God-like and due equal respect. On this view, there can be no reason to respect human life more than the life of any animal, just as there can be no reason to respect a way of life dedicated to moral excellence and care for others more than one devoted to animal pleasures and indifference to others. Dignity implies elevation, and elevation implies hierarchy; but pantheism levels everything.

In sum, for John Paul II the sense of God is essential to respect for human life. Yet according to Tocqueville, modern democracy tends to foster disbelief in, forgetfulness of, and a diminution of the idea of God.

DEMOCRACY AND INDIVIDUALISM

Another current of thought eroding respect for rights, according to John Paul II, is a selfish individualism that disclaims responsibility for others. As we have seen, some versions of liberal modernity encourage such individualism by denying or downplaying man's natural sociability. If man exists by nature in isolation from his fellows, or if the dominant element in his nature is self-interested, then his obligations to others will be considered as completely, or at least largely, conventional and will accordingly be experienced as irritating constraints on his most powerful natural desires. On Tocqueville's account, however, democracy, while it does not extinguish human sociability, certainly does constrain it considerably. Democracy, in fact, fosters an individualism that threatens man's sense of responsibility to and for others.

Following his usual method, Tocqueville sheds light on this democratic weakness by way of a comparison with an aristocratic strength; for aristocracy, he contends, tightly binds men, or at least some men, to each other by means of clearly perceived and intensely felt obligations of service. In the first place, aristocracy creates strong bonds between generations by strengthening the family as a society that exists through time. Because aristocratic laws of inheritance require that property be passed intact to the eldest son, "families remain in the same state for centuries, and often in the same place." Under such conditions, the family becomes like a little fatherland, with its own territory and history, to which one has a kind of patriotic attachment. "A man almost always knows his ancestors and respects them; he believes he already perceives his great-grandsons and he loves them." Such a man, Tocqueville contends, "willingly does his duty" to familial predecessors and successors and "frequently comes to sacrifice his personal enjoyments for beings who no longer exist or who do not yet exist." Among the living, moreover, aristocracy also unites men to those outside the family. Such a society is divided into "distinct and immobile" classes. The members of each of these classes are united by shared interests, sentiments, and habits that lead them to look upon their class as a "sort of little native country, more visible and dearer than the big one." Finally, aristocracies link men even to those outside their own classes by creating a hierarchy of ranks with reciprocal rights and obligations. Each man "always perceives higher than himself a man whose protection is necessary to him, and below he finds another whom he can call upon for cooperation." Thus, Tocqueville concludes, aristocratic men are "almost always bound in a tight manner to something that is placed outside of them, and they are often disposed to forget themselves."[13]

Democracy, however, sunders all these links. The democratic law of inheritance allows parents to divide their property among their children. As a result, estates are broken up, the family ceases to be identified permanently with a certain piece of land, and accordingly loses its hold upon the imagination as a society existing through time. As social commentators besides Tocqueville have noted, in a modern democracy the term "family" refers to the nuclear family, and the predominance of this understanding tends to isolate men from the past and the future. Furthermore, in a democracy classes of a sort remain, but their membership constantly changes as fortunes are made and lost and families rise and fall. Class identity is therefore diminished, as is the sense of commitment to those of one's class. Last of all, democracy "breaks the chain" of obedience and obligation that had linked all members of society hierarchically from "the peasant up to the king." All men now being equal, one finds a large number who have enough wealth to be self-sufficient but not enough to influence others. Such men, owing nothing to others and expecting nothing from them, think of themselves "in isolation." Tocqueville concludes: "Thus not only does democracy make each man forget his ancestors, but it hides his descendants from him and separates him from his contemporaries; it constantly leads him back toward himself and threatens finally to confine him wholly in the solitude of his own heart."[14]

This is not to say that democratic equality immediately isolates each individual and leads him to view the rest of humanity as mere instruments of, or impediments to, his own interests. Tocqueville is careful to distinguish individualism from selfishness. The former, he indicates, is a distinctively democratic proclivity that leads men to "withdraw" from society at large and to focus their attention only upon their family and friends. The latter, in contrast, is a "vice as old as the world" constituted by "a passionate and exaggerated love for self that brings man to relate everything to himself alone and to prefer himself to everything." Selfishness therefore "withers the seed of all the virtues," while individualism "at first dries up only the source of the public virtues." Nevertheless, Tocqueville adds, individualism tends "in the long term" to destroy *all* virtue and "finally" to be "absorbed in selfishness."[15] Thus, on Tocqueville's account, democracy fosters a turn of mind that, according to John Paul II, undermines our sense of obligation to others and leads us to sacrifice their rights to our own interests.

DEMOCRACY AND HEDONISM

The argument of *Evangelium Vitae* also identifies hedonism or materialism as a threat to the civilization capable of principled respect for human rights and human dignity. When human beings take physical pleasures and material goods as the core of their happiness, the deeper, and more truly human, satisfactions of morally upright action and loving self-sacrifice for others become obscured or unintelligible. We are then led to evaluate the worth of others by a utilitarian standard, judging them according to their contribution to our own or the community's material interests. At this point we are far from respecting others on the basis of their intrinsic dignity as human beings, and we will be inclined to disregard the rights of those who cannot contribute to material prosperity or whose weakness actually places demands on our own material resources.

According to the argument of *Democracy in America*, however, democracy favors just such a morally problematic materialism or hedonism. American life, Tocqueville notes, is dominated by the "passion for material well-being." For Americans, the "care of satisfying the least needs of the body and of providing the smallest comforts of life preoccupies minds universally." Observing a similar trait emerging in Europe, he concludes that such materialism is not distinctively American but rather of democratic origins. This is not to say that modern democracy gives birth to the longing for material enjoyments, which Tocqueville acknowledges is "natural and instinctive" for human beings under any social conditions.[16] Nevertheless, democracy uniquely agitates this natural desire, thus giving rise to a distinctively democratic public materialism.

The key to Tocqueville's argument is the following anthropological insight: "What attaches the human heart most keenly is not the peaceful possession of a precious object, but the imperfectly satisfied desire to possess it and the incessant fear of losing it." On this view, aristocracy discourages materialism by definitively and irrevocably settling the distribution of material enjoyments, while democracy fosters materialism by opening a ceaseless competition to win and hold on to material goods. Aristocrats, their social status fixed by law, have never "known a state different from their own, do not fear changing it," and can "hardly imagine another." They thus enjoy material pleasures without becoming obsessed with them, and their attention turns to other matters, such as the cultivation of the mind or the direction of public authority. Looking to the "lower classes" of an aristocratic society, Tocqueville sees "analogous effects produced by different causes." While nobles transcend materialism through an easy familiarity with material goods, the people transcend it through ignorance and despair of worldly comforts. Where classes are fixed, Tocqueville argues, "the people in the end become habituated to poverty like the rich to their opulence." The poor do not pine for material well-being "because they despair of acquiring it and because they are not familiar enough with it to desire it." They instead seek the consolations of piety, dwelling in imagination on the next life.[17]

Democracy, in contrast, excites the taste for material well-being by liberating and imperfectly fulfilling it. When rank is no longer established by law and custom, the possibility of upward social mobility, and the material comforts it offers, preoccupies the minds of the lower classes. Thus Tocqueville observes that while in America he never found a man "so poor that he did not cast a glance of hope and longing on the enjoyments of the rich." The desire for material goods also dominates the thoughts of the middle class in a democracy, because moderate success in acquiring material goods is not sufficient to satisfy democratic materialism. Democracy, Tocqueville notes, tends to create "a multitude of mediocre fortunes," which offer "material enjoyments" sufficient for their possessors to develop "the taste for these enjoyments," but "not enough to be content with them." Finally, even the rich in democracies remain in the grip of the materialistic passion. After all, the economic freedom and competition unleashed by democracy creates the possibility not only of upward, but also of downward, mobility. Therefore the rich cannot enjoy their material comforts without the fear of losing them. Besides, since most of the rich in a democracy begin life at a lower station, by the time they become wealthy their habits are fixed and they cannot then shake off their preoccupation with material goods. Even those democratic men who enjoy great wealth effortlessly through inheritance cannot escape this obsession, Tocqueville contends, because they are influenced by the example of the rest of the society. "Love of well-being has become the national and dominant taste." Thus the "great current of human passions bears from this direction" and "carries everything along in its course."[18]

Tocqueville is careful to add that this materialism does not directly and immediately corrupt the souls of democratic peoples. That is, it does not lead to the pursuit of extravagant or criminal pleasures. On the contrary, democratic materialism is compatible with orderly behavior and "regular mores." After all, the aforementioned uncertainty of the prosperity that democratic citizens are able to attain ensures in most cases that they will not risk any extreme indulgences. The danger posed by democratic materialism, then, seems to consist not so much in outright vice as in a certain weakness of spirit. Thus Tocqueville warns that democracy might establish "a sort of honest materialism that does not corrupt souls, but softens them and in the end quietly loosens all their tensions."[19] Nevertheless, even this softness can be understood as paving the way for the evils later discerned by John Paul II. For human beings who are preoccupied with pleasure—even if they limit themselves to legitimate pleasures—will come to view as enemies those whose neediness makes demands on them. Writing elsewhere in *Democracy in America*, Tocqueville observes another trait related to democratic materialism: a "taste for easy successes and present enjoyments."[20] Put simply, even honest materialism is averse to self-sacrifice, yet on John Paul II's account some spirit of self-sacrifice is necessary in order both to live up to the true idea of human dignity and to respect the dignity of others.

As *Democracy in America* draws to a close, Tocqueville offers a portrait of democratic man that seems to sum up his individualistic and hedonistic proclivities:

> I see an innumerable crowd of like and equal men who revolve on themselves without repose, procuring the small and vulgar pleasures with which they fill their souls. Each of them, withdrawn and apart, is like a stranger to the destiny of all the others: his children and his particular friends form the whole human species for him; as for dwelling with his fellow citizens, he is beside them, but he does not see them: he touches them and does not feel them; he exists only in himself and

for himself alone, and if a family still remains for him, one can at least say that he no longer has a native country.[21]

Such men already possess, or are primed to develop, the habits of thought that John Paul II believes underpin the contemporary crisis of respect for rights.

SELF-INTEREST WELL UNDERSTOOD

Democracy, it seems, fosters a hedonistic individualism that one might fairly characterize as Hobbesian. Nevertheless, society cannot be sustained simply on the basis of hedonistic individualism. Some morality is required, if only one based itself on hedonistic individualism. This, as we have seen, is Hobbes's solution, as well as, according to John Paul II, the solution adopted by contemporary society: a law of nature and a civil law intended to appeal to man's fundamental desire for comfortable self-preservation. *Democracy in America* suggests, however, that this is also the solution to which democratic peoples are spontaneously drawn.

In aristocracies, Tocqueville contends, members of the noble class naturally tend to conceive a "sublime idea of the duties of man." Born to authority, sheltered from necessity, and tightly bound to things outside themselves—family and class, superiors and subordinates—they come to view morality as a matter of utterly disinterested service to others. They are "pleased to profess that it is glorious to forget oneself and that it is fitting to do good without self-interest like God himself." Moreover, because public authority resides in their class, their opinions set the tone for the society as a whole. Thus in aristocratic times an emphasis on self-forgetfulness and the loveliness—as opposed to the utility—of virtue characterizes "the official doctrine . . . in the matter of morality."[22]

Democracy, in contrast, fosters a very different moral doctrine, the "doctrine of self-interest well understood," which emerges as a result of democratic moralists' efforts to accommodate democracy's powerful inclination toward hedonistic individualism. Under conditions of democratic equality, Tocqueville argues, "the imagination takes a less lofty flight and each man concentrates on himself." As a result, "moralists become frightened at this idea of sacrifice and they no longer dare to offer it to the human mind." They are instead "reduced" to emphasizing the individual utility of public spiritedness and highlighting those areas where "particular interest happens to meet the general interest and to be confounded with it." They do not speak of virtue as "beautiful" but as "useful," and do not claim that one should sacrifice for others "because it is great to do it" but because "such sacrifices are as necessary to the one who imposes them on himself as to the one who profits from them." This understanding of morality as enlightened self-interest comes to prevail generally, and it in fact penetrates so deeply into the democratic mind that even the ministers of religion present their teaching in such terms. Thus Tocqueville observes of "American preachers" that "it is often difficult to know when listening to them if the principal object of religion is to procure eternal felicity in the other world or well-being in this one."[23]

Democratic morality, then, is essentially utilitarian: it advises us to do good to others in view of the good we might expect to receive in return from them—with the "good" understood primarily, moreover, in material terms. As John Paul II reminds us, however, and as we have seen most clearly in the thought of Hobbes, such a morality does little to foster recognition of or respect for the intrinsic dignity of human beings as human beings. It instead promotes an understanding of others as tools that may be serviceable with a view to one's own self-interest. As a result, such a morality does little to encourage service rendered to the most weak among us, since they have no ability to repay our services in kind.

Democratic morality not only leaves the weak without much hope of support; it also exposes their very rights to invasion. That is, it threatens to create a society that is not only uncharitable but also unjust. For Tocqueville holds that the doctrine of self-interest well understood informs not only the good services that Americans choose to perform, but also their respect for each others' rights.[24] According to Tocqueville, then, the modern democratic man's respect for the rights of others is based on the Hobbesian calculation of chapter 13 of the *Leviathan*. Rights are to be posited and observed, or one's freedom to do all things renounced, on the basis of self-interested fear and desire: if I claim the right to do anything to secure myself, others will do the same, very possibly to my own harm or destruction. As we have observed before, such an account of rights raises the question posed by Glaucon and Adeimantus to Socrates in Plato's *Republic*: why should I be just if it seems profitable to be unjust and I can reasonably believe I will get away with injustice? Unlike Socrates or John Paul II, however, Hobbes and the doctrine of self-interest well understood can provide no principled answer.

DEMOCRATIC HUMANITARIANISM

One might respond to the preceding argument by contending that democracy solves this problem not through principle but through senti-ment. That is, while democratic moral theory can support no principled respect for the rights and dignity of the human person, democratic social conditions nevertheless foster compassionate habits that are favorable to the weak and vulnerable. Tocqueville, after all, argues that equal-ity of conditions fosters the development of mild mores. Perhaps, then, democracy can boast a natural corrective to its selfish, hedonistic individualism.

Aristocracy, as we have already seen, fosters a generous morality capable of inducing extraordinary devotions. Nevertheless, Tocqueville adds, aristocracy does not favor "mildness of mores." That is, it under-mines a sense of sympathy for the sufferings of other human beings as human beings: "for there is real sympathy only among people who are alike," and in an aristocracy "one sees those like oneself only in the mem-bers of one's caste." Sympathy therefore exists in aristocracies, but its operation is confined to a very narrow sphere. Tocqueville notes that aristocrats are often found to treat those with whom they can identify—that is, their equals—with the most refined sensitivity. Their compassion may even extend to members of the lower classes with whom they are personally acquainted, such as their own servants. At the same time, however, they can be found displaying the most startling indifference to the sufferings of the lower classes generally. Such hardness, Tocqueville insists, arises less from depravity than simple ignorance. The experi-ences, thoughts, and feelings of commoners are so alien to nobles that that the latter can "scarcely believe themselves to be a part of the same humanity." Tocqueville provides as an example Madame de Sévigné's discussion of the grievous punishments imposed on Brittany's rebellious peasants, noting that her lighthearted account shows not that she was "barbaric" but only that she "did not clearly conceive what it was to suffer when one was not a gentleman."[25]

Democracy, in contrast, expands the scope of sympathy by making most human beings in fact more alike. Aristocracy divides society into two groups, one freed from labor and with access to a very refined education, the other almost completely ignorant because completely confined to necessitous work. Democracy, however, gives rise to a primarily middle class society, a society in which almost all are compelled to work but also have access to at least some education, primarily practical in character. Having such similar experiences and aspirations, democratic men can understand each other more readily and the reach of human sympathy accordingly increases. "When ranks are almost equal in a people," Tocqueville contends

> all men having nearly the same manner of thinking and feeling, each of them can judge the sensations of all the others in a moment: he casts a rapid glance at himself; that is enough for him. There is therefore no misery he does not conceive without trouble and whose extent a secret instinct does not discover for him. It makes no difference whether it is a question of strangers or of enemies: imagination immediately puts him in their place. It mixes something personal with his pity and makes him suffer himself while the body of someone like him is torn apart.

Thus democratic men are inclined to "show a general compassion for all members of the human species."[26]

Democratic compassion, however, is not sufficient to foster the loving service for which John Paul II calls, or even a reliable respect for the dignity and rights of others. In the first place, democratic sympathy is watered down and undemanding. Tocqueville's account indicates that democracy weakens sympathy even as it expands it, rendering it much wider but much less deep than what is encountered in an aristocracy. Our "sensitivity bears on more objects" than that of our fathers, but we are not necessarily for that reason more sensitive, he notes. Indeed, Tocqueville holds that aristocrats "feel a continual and active sympathy for one another that can never be encountered to the same degree among citizens of a democracy." This should not be surprising, since democracy's humanitarianism has to remain compatible with its hedonistic individualism. Thus Tocqueville sums up the sympathy of democratic people as follows: "One does not see them inflict useless evils, and when they can relieve the sorrows of another without denying themselves much, they take pleasure in doing it."[27] Democratic compassion, it seems, does little to foster the "gift of self" through which John Paul II thinks a human being fulfills his own nature and acknowledges the dignity of others.

Indeed, Tocqueville implies that when democratic sympathy does lead to acts of positive service—as opposed to mere abstention from harm—it nevertheless retains an element of calculation, that it is conditioned, and hence constrained, by self-interest well understood. Thus in a discussion following up his account of the mildness of democratic mores, he observes that democrats tend to render aid out of a sense of their common vulnerability. "At the same time that equality of conditions makes men feel their independence," he argues, "it shows them their weakness." Equal and free, such men are "exposed to a thousand accidents, and experience is not slow to teach them that although they do not have a habitual need of assistance from others, some moment almost always arrives when they cannot do without it."[28] Again, such compassion tends to exclude those who are most in need of compassion; for it offers sympathy and support always with an eye on some potential benefit to be gained in return, and therefore sees little reason to help the weakest and most infirm, those who seem to have no material benefits to offer.

Finally, because democratic sympathy depends on the democratic citizen's perceptions and experiences of his similarity to others, it remains compatible with the most ruthless indifference towards those who can still be perceived as radically different—for example, those who suffer from extreme disabilities or debilitating illnesses, or even those of a very different culture from one's own. Such differences remain even under democratic conditions; and common experience tells us that they all too often call forth the insensitivity, and even the hostility, of otherwise decent and humane democratic citizens.

Indeed, the limitations of democratic sympathy were glaringly evident even in Tocqueville's own time. Tocqueville observes the "frightful miseries" and "cruel punishments" visited upon America's African slaves. Their hard plight, he argues, arises not only from the self-interest of the slave holders, but also from the latter's lack of sympathy. Masters, he says, feel "little pity" for slaves because they perceive slavery as "an ill that scarcely touches them." This lack of pity, moreover, follows from democratic sympathy's dependence on a sense of similarity. "Thus," Tocqueville concludes, "the same man who is full of humanity for those like him when they are at the same time his equals becomes insensitive to their sorrows as soon as equality ceases." Democratic sympathy likewise provided little protection for American Indians, who, Tocqueville notes, also suffered a kind of "tyranny" and whose "miseries," though different from those of the Africans, could nevertheless be attributed to the "same authors."[29] This is, again, not surprising, given the basis of democratic sympathy. The Indians, Tocqueville observes, lived a life that was largely alien to the agrarian, commercial, and industrial habits of most Europeans. The latter could not easily understand, and therefore could not much sympathize, with the former.

THE DANGER OF DEMOCRATIC TYRANNY

Tocqueville's references to the "tyranny" to which Africans and Native Americans were subjected indicate that the rise of democratic sympathy does not necessarily prevent grave abuses of human dignity. This is, of course, no isolated or accidental insight. *Democracy in America* famously makes the case for modern democracy's susceptibility to tyranny, which arises, Tocqueville contends, from some of democracy's deepest inclinations—inclinations, moreover, similar to those also identified by John Paul II as fostering a potentially tyrannical disregard for human rights.

We may begin by observing that democracy, on Tocqueville's account, saps the public spiritedness that would object to tyranny in principle, that is, to tyrannical denials of other people's rights. Tocqueville's democratic man, once again, is primarily a hedonistic individualist. Democratic man is therefore reminiscent of Lockean man as he appears in the *Two Treatises*. As we have observed, however, Lockean man, preoccupied with his own comfortable self-preservation, is not terribly exercised by abuses of the rights of others so long as his own interests remain untouched. The same is true of Tocqueville's democratic man, and this trait arises precisely from his individualism and hedonism.

Democratic individualism, Tocqueville argues, is an invitation to despotism. Despotism favors and cultivates the isolation, indifference, and selfishness of citizens. The despot "readily pardons the governed for not loving him, provided that they do not love each other." Democracy, however, favors, as we have already seen, an individualism that gradually shades into outright selfishness. "Thus the vices to which despotism gives birth are precisely those that equality favors," and accordingly despotism is "particularly to be feared in democratic times."[30]

Democratic hedonism leads to the same consequences by a slightly different route. Dedicated to the pursuit of material comforts, democratic citizens devote most of their attention to the economic activity that is the most direct means to their coveted end. As a result, they are unwilling to spend time on their public responsibilities, the exercise of which "appears to them a distressing contretemps that distracts them from their industry." Attention to the common good through vigilant political activism is to them a "useless work" on which "they cannot waste their precious time." Under such conditions, Tocqueville notes, "an ambitious, able" ruler will find "the way open to every usurpation." So long as he ensures that "material interests prosper," the citizens will "release him" from every other obligation.[31]

At this point one might object that the despotism of which democratic men are inclined to be so tolerant does not necessarily amount to tyranny. After all, the term "despotism," at least in its traditional usage in political theory, does not necessarily carry the same moral baggage as the term "tyranny." The English word "despot" is derived from the Greek word for the master of slaves. Yet Aristotle, for example, held that some forms of mastery were morally justifiable. Tyranny, in contrast, he defined as a form of bad, disordered, or perverted rule, since it seeks not the common good but only the interest of the ruler.[32] This distinction, though obscured by modern political thought's emphasis on freedom, can nevertheless still be observed in modern authors. Thus in *On Liberty* John Stuart Mill speaks of tyranny as an evil, but concedes that despotism may be a permissible mode of government for populations incapable of improvement through rational discussion.[33] In sum, despotism traditionally refers merely to rule by force, while tyranny refers to bad rule, and we might well suspect that Tocqueville—who was both conversant with the history of political philosophy and a very well-informed contemporary of Mill—uses the terms with this distinction in mind.[34]

We can respond to this objection by observing that tyranny and despotism, though perhaps theoretically distinct, are nevertheless somewhat practically related. After all, for imperfect human beings, rule by force without the reasonable input of others is likely to lead to abusive or bad behaviors. Thus Tocqueville suggests that the despotism he fears will be tyrannical as well. He notes that in a nation under the influence of democratic materialism, the "despotism of factions is no less to be dreaded" than "that of one man." Such factions, he continues, in "dispos[ing] of all things according to their whim," will "change laws and tyrannize at will over mores."[35] Since Tocqueville uses the term "mores" to refer in part to a nation's moral convictions, he seems to fear that despotism inclines to evildoing.[36]

If democratic citizens are willing to tolerate tyranny when it does not harm their own interests, are they willing to collude in it actively in order to promote their own interests? The reality of the latter danger is evident to anyone possessing even a passing familiarity with Tocqueville's most famous work. Tyranny of the majority is a major theme in *Democracy in America*, the work to which the term owes, if not its origin, then certainly its popularization. To some extent the ultimate origins of this problem are to be sought not in the democratic social state but in the human condition. Given a flawed human nature, an impulse toward tyranny can manifest itself in any regime. Thus, when Tocqueville introduces his discussion of majority tyranny, he defends its possibility as follows:

> What therefore is a majority taken collectively, if not an individual who has opinions and most often interests contrary to another individual that one names the minority? Now, if you accept that one man vested with omnipotence can abuse it against his adversaries, why not accept the same thing for a majority? Have men changed in character by being united? Have they become more patient of obstacles by becoming stronger? As for me, I cannot believe it; and I shall never grant to several the power of doing everything that I refuse to a single one of those like me.[37]

While the inclination of a majority to behave tyrannically certainly is not created by democracy, democracy does foster habits of thought that exacerbate this natural human tendency. For, on Tocqueville's account, a perverse but inevitable consequence of democracy's preoccupation with equality is to diminish the worth of the individual and magnify the apparent majesty of the majority. Once men become equal, he contends, in comparison to the mass each individual comes to seem utterly insignificant, even to himself. "[E]ach citizen, having become like all the others, is lost in the crowd," and one can no longer see anything but "the vast and magnificent image of the people itself." Thus "men in democratic times" naturally conceive "a very high opinion of the privileges of society and a very humble idea of the rights of the individual."[38]

As society's representative and the custodian of its "privileges," the majority comes to participate in its magnificence. In fact, on Tocqueville's argument democracy fosters a respect for the majority that borders on veneration. Democrats, he observes, defer not only to the majority's right to exercise public authority, but even tend to believe that its decisions must be right. When conditions of equality prevail and most men are similar, when there are no outstanding examples of intellectual superiority, nothing is more natural than to believe that truth and justice must lie on the side of the majority. Thus Tocqueville holds that democracies tend to submit to the "moral empire of the majority," which is "founded in part on the idea that there is more enlightenment and wisdom in many men united than in one," or, in short, on "the theory of equality applied to intellects."[39] The individual in democratic times doubts his own judgment when he is tempted to think that the majority has erred, and, in addition, its powers of ostracism dissuade him from speaking out even when he has sufficient strength of mind to hold to his own opinion. This influence over opinion, Tocqueville suggests, renders the power of the majority immense, with consequences that are "dire and dangerous for the future."[40]

Chapter 8

CONCLUSION

The preceding chapters of this book have examined various strains of modern political thought in light of John Paul II's argument in *Evangelium Vitae*. This examination suggests that, judged according to the pope's principles, the various manifestations of liberal modernity, from the most radical and extreme to the more qualified and moderate, are seriously and dangerously deficient. John Paul II observes an eclipse of respect for human rights and human dignity in the contemporary societies of the developed West, an eclipse he traces to a hedonistic individualism that has come to dominate such societies. Such hedonistic individualism, however, as well as its tyrannical implications, are already present and openly affirmed at the dawn of liberal modernity in the thought of Thomas Hobbes. Later articulations of liberal modernity—such as the political thought of John Locke, David Hume, and the American founders—accept Hobbes's hedonistic individualism to some extent while trying, at the same time, to qualify it with various religious or humanitarian elements. As we have seen, however, such qualifying elements are in each case insufficiently central to correct the morally corrosive aspects of Hobbesian modernity and provide an adequate foundation for human dignity. Indeed, Tocqueville's account of modern democracy suggests that the moral and intellectual currents the pope thinks undermine the culture of rights are rooted in the democratic social state itself. Thus it would seem that what the pope terms the "culture of death" is not merely the result of some recent perversion of modern liberal principles, and accordingly that his moral critique of modern western societies is one that goes to their very foundations.

THE POPE AND THE ENLIGHTENMENT

There is also reason to believe that John Paul II was well aware of the radical nature of this critique, as we would expect of a man of his intellectual sophistication and philosophic erudition. In his writings the pope nowhere explicitly undertakes a detailed critique of the bodies of thought examined in the previous chapters, a critique which this book has rather constructed primarily on the basis of the argument of *Evangelium Vitae*. Nevertheless, his last published work—*Memory and Identity*, the book-length interview that appeared the month of his death—confirms, indirectly and in broad terms if not in detail, this book's reading of his thought as a critique of the modern liberal project. What this book has termed "liberal modernity" is a product of the philosophic movement known as the Enlightenment. Certainly Hobbes, Locke, and Hume are commonly regarded as Enlightenment thinkers. Certainly the political order established by the American founders, as well as the democratic society analyzed by Tocqueville, are commonly regarded as offshoots in action of Enlightenment philosophy. Yet in *Memory and Identity* John Paul II speaks of the Enlightenment as an evil and a source of evil, as flawed in theory and therefore productive of abuse in practice. In the book's opening pages, the pope concedes that the Enlightenment "has yielded many positive fruits." Nevertheless, he immediately reveals a more fundamental negative judgment of the Enlightenment by adding that a capacity to yield positive fruits "is actually characteristic of evil," which on the Catholic view is understood as privation but "never a total absence of good."[1] A few pages later he suggests that the most egregious modern violations of human dignity are attributable to the influence of the Enlightenment. Thus he reveals that he has "become more and more convinced that the ideologies of evil"—that is, the murderous totalitarian movements of the twentieth century—are "profoundly rooted in the history of European philosophical thought," and in this connection he mentions the European Enlightenment.[2]

In addition, the specific contours of the pope's critique of the Enlightenment in *Memory and Identity* parallel the critique of liberal modernity offered in the preceding chapters. Recall that according to the pope's argument in *Evangelium Vitae* human life is fully realized in man's embrace of his vocation to love and serve others, a vocation that is exemplified in the sacrificial death of Christ himself. A root of the culture of death, then, is a refusal to love, a turning away from man's supreme good and therefore to more limited goods, like material comfort and pleasure, in the pursuit of which men eventually come to violate each other's rights. In *Memory and Identity*, however, John Paul II suggests that the Enlightenment was characterized by a rejection of Christ, and therefore, by implication, of the vocation to love. "The rejection of Christ," he contends, "entered European thought" during "the era of the Enlightenment," a movement that, "in all its different forms," was "opposed to what Europe had become as a result of evangelization." This is not to say that the Enlightenment was simply an atheistic movement, the pope hastens to add. "Its exponents," he says, "were rather like Paul's listeners at the Aeropagus": they did not reject the notion of a supreme being, but they did reject the God who "revealed himself by becoming man" and by "giving his life for men."[3] That is, the Enlightenment rejected the God of the gospel, the God of love. This rejection is an evil, the pope contends, in the strict Thomist sense: the "absence of a good that ought to be present in a given being." Man, as a being created in God's image and likeness and "redeemed by Christ from sin," ought to possess the good of "participation in the nature and life of God himself." Thus in rejecting Christ the Enlightenment tended to cut man off from that which "guarantees him the possibility of attaining to the fullness of his humanity." Moreover, *Memory and Identity*, like *Evangelium Vitae*, suggests that this denial of love as the perfection of man's nature leads in the end to open injustice of the most grievous sort. Thus the pope indicates that the Enlightenment's rejection of Christ "opened" up a "path" that "would lead toward the devastating experiences of evil which were to follow"—that is, to the unheard of disregard for human dignity manifested by the "ideologies of evil" of the twentieth century. It is worth noting in addition that, just as *Evangelium Vitae* presents the "culture of death" as a new development arising from the spread of mistaken understandings of the human good, rather than merely a product of ordinary human depravity, so *Memory and Identity* credits the Enlightenment's rejection of Christ with opening a path to evil "in a qualitatively new and previously unknown way, at least on such a scale."[4] In every age, even in the most publicly pious ones, human beings have refused the vocation to love; yet the Enlightenment's novel contribution, it would seem, was to turn the dismissal of love into a public philosophy, and therefore to lay the intellectual and moral foundations of the culture of death that has emerged in the societies erected on Enlightenment principles.

In *Evangelium Vitae*, John Paul II also suggests that the culture of death is rooted not only in a repudiation of love but also in a more general loss of the sense of God as the supreme good and as the source of the moral law and its objective validity. In *Memory and Identity* he finds in Enlightenment thought a similar loss with similar consequences. The Enlightenment, he contends, was prepared by the thought of Descartes, and in particular by his radical reorientation of philosophy—away from a preoccupation with being, and especially with "God as fully Self-sufficient Being" and as the ground of all created being, and to a concern with the thinking subject or with the "content of human consciousness." This turn—which is evident in Descartes's celebrated point of departure, "I think therefore I am"—exerted a powerful influence on subsequent European philosophy, which tended to become a "science of pure thought" according to which the human mind enjoyed priority over being understood as existing independently of it.[5]

Such an approach to philosophy, however, could not help but lead to a diminution of God, or rather of man's idea of God. Indeed, the Cartesian logic of the Enlightenment reduced God to a mere "idea," an "element of human consciousness," rather than the ultimate cause of all being, intelligibility, and goodness. As a result of this reduction of God, however, "the foundations of the 'philosophy of evil' also collapsed," for evil can only be understood as a real, intelligible phenomenon "in relation to good and, in particular, in relation to God, the Supreme Good." Because of the absence of God as supreme good and supreme being, or because of the insistence on the philosophic priority of the content of human consciousness, man came to be seen as "alone: alone as creator of his own history and his own civilization; alone as one who decides what is good and what is bad." Yet this understanding opens the door to what the pope, in *Evangelium Vitae*, presents as the most egregious consequences of the culture of death. For, in the words of *Memory and Identity*, if "man can decide by himself, without God, what is good and what is bad, he can also determine that a group of people is to be annihilated." Hence the pope's suggestion that Enlightenment philosophy prepared the radical evils carried out by Nazis and Communists in the twentieth century.[6] This is as much as to say, however, that the worst examples of modernity's indifference to human dignity are less a perversion of modernity's fundamental principles than a consequence of them.[7]

This is not to say that the thinkers of the Enlightenment, the intellectual architects of liberal modernity, intended such consequences, that they sought a direct leap into complete relativism. Rather, as the pope notes, European traditions of thought, "especially those of the Enlightenment period," continued to recognize the "need" for some "criterion" by which to "regulate" man's use of his "freedom." Nevertheless, he adds, the "criterion adopted" has been one of "utility or pleasure." According to John Paul II, drawing on the "Aristotelian-Thomistic tradition," the good is properly understood as threefold. It includes the moral or just good (*bonum honestum*), the useful good (*bonum utile*), and the pleasurable good (*bonum delectabile*), with the first being understood as the most authoritative: the "*bonum honestum*" is "the first and fundamental dimension of good." European traditions of thought influenced by the Enlightenment, however, have adopted a utilitarianism that "ignores" this "first and fundamental" good and assumes that "man tends essentially toward his own interest or that of the group to which he belongs," that "the aim of human action is personal or corporate advantage." On this view, the pope observes, pleasure has been "somehow emancipated" from its subordination to the moral good and has become "both a good and an end in itself," and man is understood to seek "pleasure above all else, not the *honestum*."[8] As John Paul II suggests in *Evangelium Vitae*, however, and as we have seen repeatedly in the leading examples of modern liberal thought, a public morality erected on such utilitarian foundations can provide no sure support for human dignity and human rights. For its reduction of morality to enlightened self-interest leaves man with no reason to obey the moral law when there is no material gain in view. This in turn leaves the weak, or those who have little of material worth to offer, vulnerable. Regimes established on such principles remain persistently susceptible to serious violations of human rights. Thus, as the pope observes in *Memory and Identity*, even after having rejected and defeated the "ideologies of evil" that had justified mass "extermination" of innocent human beings, the "democratically elected parliaments" of the western nations almost immediately embraced "the legal extermination of human beings conceived but unborn."[9]

Memory and Identity, then, openly confirms what we have inferred from an examination of Hobbes, Locke, Hume, the American founding, and Tocqueville's account of democracy in light of *Evangelium Vitae*: namely, that for John Paul II liberal modernity, or the political project of the Enlightenment, is fundamentally flawed, that it is established on errors in theory that lead to evil in practice, that its effort to organize human life without reference to the supreme good leads, despite its proponents' humane intentions, to a susceptibility to the gravest evils. Enlightened modernity, moreover, seems to lack the intellectual resources to correct its own problematic inclinations, so that it is necessary to return once more to premodern, pre-Enlightenment philosophy if we are to extricate ourselves from the "culture of death." This the pope suggests rather bluntly when he remarks, in *Memory and Identity*, "If we wish to speak rationally about good and evil, we have to return to Saint Thomas Aquinas, that is, to the philosophy of being."[10]

FUTILE CONFLICT OR FRUITFUL TENSION?

One might object to this book's argument on the practical grounds that it sets up a futile (at best) and counterproductive (at worst) hostility between Catholicism and modernity. The preceding chapters contend that John Paul II's critique of modernity goes to its very roots, holding that liberal modernity contains serious and dangerous errors in its very philosophic foundations. Yet liberal modernity appears to be the most powerful force in the world. It seems to have transformed, or at least to be in the process of transforming, societies everywhere, with no signs of receding or reversing itself. Is it not then the case, one might ask, that the depth of John Paul's critique renders his thought simply irrelevant to liberal modernity, and hence irrelevant to the world in which we are fated to live? Given the radical character of his critique, should we not conclude that John Paul II has set up himself—and, by extension, the Catholic tradition that he represents—as the enemy of liberal modernity, just as the liberal commentators noted in chapter 1 suspected and claimed? And if this is the case, why shouldn't liberal modernity simply ignore or resist what he has to say?

In response, I would contend that the situation need not be presented in such absolutely conflictual terms. In the first place, we may note that although John Paul II is undoubtedly a radical critic of liberal modernity, it does not follow that he must view himself as its enemy. A critic, after all, may be animated by friendly intentions. Here a comparison to Tocqueville may prove illuminating. In the "Notice" that introduces volume 2 of *Democracy in America*, he admits that he "often" addresses "severe words" to the "democratic societies" emerging in Europe and North America. He nevertheless denies that such severity proceeds from hostility: "it is because I was not an adversary of democracy that I wanted to be sincere with it." Tocqueville's severity, then, seeks not to persuade men to reject democracy, but to bring its defects to light so that they might be corrected or ameliorated. Tocqueville declines to set himself up as democracy's enemy in part for practical reasons: he regards the "democratic revolution" the world is undergoing "as an irresistible fact against which it would be neither desirable nor wise to struggle."[11]

One may discern a similar disposition in John Paul II. His pontificate, he repeatedly insisted, was informed by the spirit of the Second Vatican Council, and especially by that of *Gaudium et Spes*, in the drafting of which he played a critical role.[12] Yet at Vatican II the Council Fathers seem to have come to the same conclusion that Tocqueville had reached a hundred thirty years earlier: that modernity is an accomplished fact, and that therefore a simply confrontational posture toward modernity is not a productive one. Thus, John Paul II suggests in *Memory and Identity*, the "Council's exposition of doctrine adopted a deliberately non-polemical stance" and "chose instead," following Christian practice "from the time of the Apostles," to pursue a "process of inculturation."

The Church chose, in other words, to recast its presentation of its teaching in terms more intelligible to modern man, a decision that implies a certain respect and even friendship for modernity. "Taking their cue from the Council," therefore, "Christians can engage with the modern world and enter into a constructive dialogue with it."[13]

More specifically, the Council can be understood as undertaking a kind of "turn to man," or an effort to take man as the beginning point of the Church's effort to address the modern world. This, too, can be understood as a decision to accommodate a cultural reality already recognized by Tocqueville. In an aristocracy, the hierarchical social and political arrangements accustom most men to looking up. This, combined with the wretched material conditions most men endure, fosters an inclination to direct the mind to heaven. Equality, however, encourages a very different outlook. Freed from their feudal obligations, and able through work to better their economic situation, democratic men are, as we have already noted, preoccupied with their individual interests. And when they lift their gaze from themselves they look not above themselves to heaven but merely beyond themselves to the human race. Thus Tocqueville claims that democratic poetry will take man as its theme, since "in the long term democracy turns the imagination away from all that is external to man to fix it only on man."[14] If one is to speak to modern man about God, then, he must begin by speaking to him about himself. Although this starting point is dictated by the character of the prevailing culture and not necessarily by the character of Christian revelation itself, it is not for that reason unworkable. After all, insofar as man is created in the image and likeness of God, and directed by his deepest longings to God, man can be a tolerable point of departure for theology. At any rate, we can see that even in his critique of liberal modernity John Paul II follows Vatican II in accommodating modern man's preoccupation with himself. Hence his extensive use of terms familiar to modern ears, such as rights, freedom, and self-realization or self-actualization. Hence his care in *Evangelium Vitae* and elsewhere to present the moral law *not* as a heteronomy, or something simply imposed on human nature, but as the path by which man perfects his humanity, realizes his destiny, and attains his happiness.

It would not be fair to Tocqueville or John Paul II, however, to suggest that they disclaim being enemies of modernity out of the merely pragmatic consideration that modernity is a brute fact that they are powerless to resist. Rather, both find that modernity contains, despite its flaws, something redemptive. As *Democracy in America* draws to its close, Tocqueville remarks that he is tempted to regret the passing of aristocracy, because its unequal conditions made possible a greatness in some men that is not to be found in modern democracy. Nevertheless, he concedes that democracy, though "less elevated" than aristocracy, is "more just," insofar as it ameliorates the condition of most human beings. And "its justice makes for its greatness and its beauty."[15] Similarly, in *Memory and Identity* John Paul II acknowledges a certain goodness in modernity. This concession is made even as he asserts his criticism in no uncertain terms: as we have seen, he characterizes the Enlightenment as evil and a source of evil only while at the same time conceding that it has also "yielded many positive fruits."[16]

What, precisely, does John Paul II find good about the Enlightenment or about liberal modernity? Here we must revert once again to the notion of a turn to man, and in a way that seems, at first glance, to reveal a contradiction in the pope's thought. In *Memory and Identity*, John Paul II claims that postmodern thinkers err in rejecting the Enlightenment's "humanism."[17] He must, then, view this humanism as something worthy of approval. In *Fides et Ratio* he says even more straightforwardly that "[m]odern philosophy clearly has the great merit of focusing attention upon man."[18] Such remarks at first seem puzzling. Have we not already seen that John Paul II criticizes the Enlightenment precisely for its turn to man, that is, for its preoccupation with human subjectivity to the exclusion of the philosophy of being? The pope, however, does not contradict himself; for a particular "turn" *to* something may be regarded as either good or bad depending on what one is turning *from*. This requires some explanation. For John Paul II, the Enlightenment's humanism can be understood as good, because a certain humanism need not be based on a turning from God but instead as "profoundly rooted in the Christian tradition."[19] More specifically, he indicates that the Enlightenment, or liberal modernity, is to be praised for its emphasis on the rights of man, for fostering "a better understanding of human rights." Modernity's popularization of the idea of human rights does not in itself entail a turning from God, because "human rights" have "divine foundations." The notion that men possess rights is, for the pope, "rooted in" the Christian understanding of "the nature of man created by God in his own image." This assertion of human rights did, however, require "leaving behind the traditions of feudalism."[20]

For John Paul II, then, the modern "turn to man" is a mistake to the extent that it takes the form of a turning from God as the supreme good, but it is to be welcomed to the extent that it takes the form of a turning from "the traditions of feudalism." Feudalism is problematic for the pope, we surmise, because it is not "humanistic," because the idea of human dignity is alien to it: in its emphasis on class and rank, it obscures the idea that human beings *as human beings* are to be accorded a certain respect. On the feudal worldview, "rights" are privileges attached to certain social ranks, and "dignity" is a quality exclusively possessed by aristocrats. The Enlightenment, or modern liberalism, then, is to be credited with revitalizing, or perhaps even with effectively bringing to light for the first time, the idea that every human being, as a human being, has rights and dignity that must be respected—an idea implicit in the Bible but obscured for many centuries by the aristocratic social state in which Christianity had to operate. Hence the pope remarks that it "is striking how often the logic of Enlightenment led to a profound rediscovery of the truths contained in the Gospel."[21]

Here we are once more struck by how John Paul II's assessment of the Enlightenment finds an echo in Tocqueville's account of modern democracy. For Tocqueville explicitly acknowledges and explains the feudal antihumanism to which the pope seems implicitly to refer. As we noted in chapter 7, aristocrats have an aversion to general ideas or a passion for particularity, an inclination arising from their constant experience of difference and inequality. As a result, Tocqueville argues, it comes to appear that "there are as many distinct humanities as there are classes," and "losing sight of the general bond that brings all together in the vast bosom of the human race, one ever views only some men, not man." Thus even the "profound and vast geniuses" of the ancient aristocratic world remained blind to the idea of equal human rights, and "it was necessary that Jesus Christ come to earth to make it understood that all members of the human species are naturally alike and equal."[22] Tocqueville's observations about aristocratic particularism and how it creates the impression of "distinct humanities," however, apply to all aristocracies, and not only those of the ancient world. Thus his account implies that even after Christ came and established the equal dignity of all human beings as human beings this truth would tend at first to remain obscure, falling as it had upon the inhospitable intellectual soil of the aristocratic social state. As a result, despite the undoubted sincerity of their piety, the feudal societies of the middle ages had at best an uncertain appreciation of the dignity and rights of the human person.

Taking into account, then, both the pope's criticism and commendation of the Enlightenment, or of liberal modernity, we may summarize his position as follows. The Enlightenment was correct to focus on man and even on the individual, forcefully asserting that human beings possess a certain dignity and enjoy certain rights simply by virtue of their humanity. It erred theoretically, however, in the anthropology or account of human nature it posited as the basis of human rights and human dignity. For John Paul II, the dignity and rights of man are properly understood as rooted in man's status as a being created in God's image and likeness and possessing a divine vocation to love, to share in the life of God by living in accordance with the moral law and ultimately by the gift of self. For the Enlightenment and liberal modernity, man is a fundamentally self-interested and hedonistic being whose rights are derived from his self-regarding desires. His dignity and rights are not intrinsic to his lofty nature—for on the modern understanding man does not have a very lofty nature—but are instead merely posited as part of a mutual nonaggression pact among selfish individuals, individuals who agree to respect each other's rights with nothing else in view but the security of their own individual interests. On the pope's view the Enlightenment account is not only inadequate but ultimately hostile to a principled respect for human dignity and human rights.

As this discussion suggests, John Paul II, though deeply critical of liberal modernity, was nevertheless reconciled to it and to some extent sympathetic to it. Liberal modernity therefore need not view him as an enemy to be ignored or resisted. Still, the partisan of liberal modernity might respond with the following further objection. The preceding argument shows only that John Paul II did not understand himself as an enemy of liberal modernity, but this does not mean that we should accept him as our friend. We may grant that he sincerely wishes to be our friend, but he is in fact that most repellent sort of potential friend—the person who seeks our friendship in order to change us, to better us according to his own lights. And in this case his lights are very different from ours. True, he shares our commitment to humanism, freedom, rights, and dignity, but his understanding of their foundations is alien to our way of thinking and in fact imposes demands upon us that we do not want. For the pope's version of human dignity not only endows us with inalienable rights but also saddles us with great obligations—to love others even to the point of gift of self, to respect the moral law even to the point of martyrdom. The very point of liberal modernity was, in Hobbes's words, to establish the moral law on such "a foundation, as passion not mistrusting, may not seek to displace."[23] While he uses terms with which we are familiar, however, John Paul II gives them a moral meaning that our passions must mistrust and even reject. Thus modern liberal man must regard the pope as an enemy, even if a well-intentioned one.

Perhaps we could answer this objection by appealing to the modern virtue of openness. Liberal modernity prides itself on its openness. Rejecting what it views as the dogmatic intolerance of past ages, it claims to be receptive even to the wisdom of contemporary cultures that are neither modern nor liberal. Couldn't liberal modernity's openness extend to listening sympathetically to the pope? Of course, this would represent a considerable challenge, given the radical character of his critique. It may be, however, that liberal modernity needs to rise to this challenge. It may be that liberal modernity cannot live up to its own highest aspirations—for freedom with justice, or for a principled respect for the rights and dignity of all—without displaying that kind of openness that liberal modernity seems to find most difficult: openness to its own past, specifically to the tradition of thought that John Paul II represents.

Here we may fruitfully recur one last time to Tocqueville, whose thought suggests that modernity must for its own good learn to be open to its premodern past. Such a spirit generally animates *Democracy in*

America, which repeatedly returns to aristocracy in order to bring to light modern democracy's deficiencies—again, not with a view to rejecting modern democracy, but to correct its problematic tendencies in the hopes of realizing a democratic modernity in which human dignity and freedom will flourish. More specifically, *Democracy in America* anticipates John Paul II's argument that modern society needs Christianity and Christian morality. As we have seen in chapter 7, John Paul II's account of the contemporary "culture of death" and Tocqueville's account of modern democracy diagnose the same basic ills: both see a hedonistic individualism that undermines commitment to morality and respect for others and that finally paves the way for tyranny. Both, moreover, prescribe similar remedies. John Paul II offers a religious teaching that asserts the primacy of moral values in opposition to the materialism and individualism of contemporary culture. Similarly, Tocqueville presents "religion" as the force that can constructively resist democracy's dangerous inclinations to an excessive "love of material enjoyments" and isolation of citizens from each other by elevating the "soul toward regions much superior to those of the senses" and by "imposing some duties toward the human species or in common with it."[24] John Paul II insists on the objectivity of moral values as rooted in God in opposition to a relativism that is in principle open to tyranny. Similarly, Tocqueville praises American Christianity for rendering "everything certain and fixed in the moral world" and forbidding the tyrannical and "impious maxim" that "everything is permitted in the interest of society."[25] Finally, Tocqueville, like John Paul II, presents this politically and morally salutary religion not as artificially constraining but instead as completing and perfecting human nature, and hence as supporting a genuinely human flourishing. Tocqueville presents man as a religious being, one whose nature aspires beyond nature to the "infinite, immaterial, and beautiful."[26] Thus he concludes that American Christianity provides the soul with a necessary nourishment that is generally unavailable in the rest of the culture.[27] Indeed, Tocqueville even goes so far as to approve Christianity's role in sustaining a morality of love. He praises as a "magnificent expression" the Christian idea that "one ought to do good to those like oneself out of love of God." In light of this teaching, Tocqueville suggests, man "freely associates himself" with God's design, "sacrificing his particular interests to the admirable order of things," expecting "no other recompense than the pleasure of contemplating it." [28] Even this demanding moral teaching, Tocqueville suggests, builds upon human nature rather than doing violence to it; for it corresponds to and fosters the "disinterested and unreflective sparks that are natural to man."[29]

We can say, then, that by mounting his critique of liberal modernity—and even more by presenting the morality of the Gospel as an alternative to liberal modernity's most problematic tendencies—John Paul II is simply doing the work that Tocqueville suggests is the duty of "honest and enlightened men" living within modern democracies: "raising up souls and keeping them turned toward Heaven," fostering "a taste for the infinite, a sentiment of greatness, and a love of immaterial pleasures."[30] And if someone should press the objection that the pope, in undertaking this work, has introduced ideas that are alien to the philosophic tradition of liberal modernity, we may further note that even Tocqueville indicates that this is necessary. For him, the well-being of modern democracy requires an appeal to religion. Yet, as we have seen in chapter 7, Tocqueville finds that democracy does not spontaneously support religious sentiments. On the contrary, he suggests that religion is in some sense alien to modern democracy: democrats, he says, should "preserve" religion "carefully as the most precious inheritance from aristocratic centuries."[31] Few serious people of any moral or political persuasion, however, would earnestly maintain that Tocqueville should be regarded as an enemy of liberal modernity, that the aims animating his thought are so alien to our own that he should be ignored at least and positively rejected at most. It is difficult to see, then, why anyone should take such a position with regard to John Paul II.

Nevertheless, the determined critic might insist that by advancing such arguments both John Paul II and Tocqueville, regardless of the latter's widespread intellectual respectability, prove their irrelevance to a modern world that, embracing secularism, has no need of the transcendent, and that, organizing its life around enlightened self-interest, has no need for love. In response, then, we may conclude by identifying two considerations supporting the relevance of the pope's thought to liberal modernity, or suggesting that liberal modernity genuinely needs the moral teaching that the pope is proposing.

As was noted in the preface, some commentators have taken the terrorist attacks of September 11, 2001 as evidence of religion's political and moral unwholesomeness. Religion, they suggest, inspires an irrational fanaticism that leads to violence. Examining such events in a different light, however, we might equally contend that they demonstrate society's real need for the morality of love that John Paul II offers. For whatever else they suggest, events like those of September 11 surely demonstrate that the world remains a very dangerous place—in which, we might add, people are moved to violence not only by religion, but also by national or ethnic solidarities or economic interests, sometimes invoking religion as a convenient justification rather than responding to it as the genuine motivation. The self-sacrificing virtues will therefore remain necessary to the defense of any society. As long as some people and communities resort to violence aggressively and unjustly, some members of all communities—such as police, firefighters, and soldiers—will have to expose themselves to the effects of violence in order to contain it and restore a just order. Put more bluntly, some must risk and even sacrifice their lives so that their fellow citizens can dwell in peace and security. The intellectual tradition upon which John Paul II draws can affirm the goodness of such sacrifices even for those who must make them: "Greater love has no man than this, that a man lay down his life for his friends," says the gospel.[32] The tradition of liberal modernity, which understands man as a being animated primarily by individual self-interest, cannot.

Liberal societies, of course, seek something more than their mere survival. They seek to survive on certain terms. They nobly aspire to affirm and respect the dignity and rights of every human being as a human being. Yet there is a kind of contradiction in liberal modernity that impedes their ability to do so: liberal modernity's anthropology undermines its morality. "What is man that thou art mindful of him, and the son of man that thou dost care for him?" the psalmist asks God. We might pose the same question to ourselves. What is my fellow man that I should respect his dignity and rights, even when I find it costly? Indeed, what am I that I should sacrifice my own interests in order to treat others with justice and even with love? As we have seen, John Paul II's answer to such questions draws upon the psalmist's answer to the question posed to God: "thou hast made" man "little less than God, and dost crown him with glory and honor."[33] My fellow man is created in God's image and likeness, and thus his very nature calls for my reverence. I am created in God's image and likeness, and thus I realize and perfect my own nature through my love for others.

Liberal modernity, however, gives another answer to the question of man, one that is far less persuasive with a view to sustaining respect for human dignity. According to that tradition, my fellow man is, like me, fundamentally a self-interested individual, a seeker of bodily pleasures, a producer and consumer of material goods. He is also, like me, frightened and vulnerable, threatened by a human environment in which no man cares for any other. Though self-interested, he is therefore, like me, willing to deal, open to a truce. Thus we agree to posit human dignity and human rights in order to safeguard ourselves. On this view, dignity and rights are not truths about human nature but merely fictions created with a view to self-interest. Such a solution is problematic, however. It asks us to treat with special reverence a creature that we at the same time suggest is no more than a clever animal. It asks us to affirm the nobility of an ethic that is transparently nothing more than what Nietzsche called slave morality—a code claiming a lofty purpose, but in fact merely devised to protect the weak, those who reject exploitation not out of principle but because they fear they cannot get away with it.[34] Such a morality can give us no good reason to reject exploitation when we think we can get away with it. These considerations invite us to consider whether human dignity might be better established if understood as inherent in human nature conceived in elevated terms rather than merely as posited in the interests of a human nature understood in low terms. They invite us, in other words, to entertain the possibility that John Paul II's teaching is not only necessary to the survival of liberal societies but to the fulfillment of the highest aspirations they proclaim.

NOTES

Front Matter

1 John Paul II, *Veritatis Splendor* (Boston: Pauline Books & Media, 1993), sec. 99.

2 Walker Percy, *Signposts in a Strange Land* (New York: Farrar, Straus, & Giroux, 1991), 162.

3 Quoted in Leo Strauss, *Natural Right and History* (Chicago: University of Chicago Press, 1953), 247.

Chapter 1

1 Duncan Currie, "Misunderstanding John Paul II," *Weekly Standard*, 18 April 2005, 15.

2 George Weigel, *Witness to Hope: The Biography of John Paul II* (Cliff Street Books, 1999), 4.

3 Discussions of John Paul II's role in fostering the fall of communism can be found in Weigel's *Witness to Hope*, as well as in his *The Final Revolution: The Resistance Church and the Fall of Communism* (New York: Oxford University Press, 2003). This topic also receives considerable attention in Jonathan Kwitny, *Man of the Century: The Life and Times of John Paul II* (New York: Henry Holt, 1997), and in Carl Bernstein and Marco Politi, *His Holiness: John Paul II and the Hidden History of Our Time* (New York: Doubleday, 1996).

4 "Pope John Paul II: Keeper of the Flock for a Quarter of a Century," *The New York Times*, 3 April 2005, sec. 1, p. 46.

5 Peter J. Boyle, "A Hard Faith," *New Yorker*, 16 May 2005, 54–65. Other examples of such liberal commentary include the following. Michael Sean Winters claimed that "John Paul II decided to confront modernity" ("After John Paul II: History Test," *The New Republic*, 18 April 2005, 17). Also, the *Economist* in "The Legacy of a Pope Who Changed History" (2 April 2005, 1) presented John Paul II as "a pope who resisted pressures to 'modernise' the church's values."

6 Joseph Bottum, "John Paul the Great: 1920–2005," *Weekly Standard*, 18 April 2005, 20.

7 George Weigel, "Mourning and Remembrance," *Wall Street Journal*, 4 April 2005, sec. A, p. 14. Similar examples of the conservative view abound. Michael Novak suggested that those who charged that "the Pope 'failed' to bring the Catholic Church into 'modernity'" were confusing "'modernity' with the least noble practices of the ironically named 'progressives' of Europe and America" ("John Paul the Great," *National Review*, 25 April 2005, 36). In addition, the editorial, "A Man for All Seasons," presented John Paul II as a man "eminently comfortable with modernity—even while he refused to accept modernity's most shallow assumptions" (*Wall Street Journal* 4 April 2005, sec. A, p. 14).

8 Quoted in Weigel, *Witness to Hope*, 5.

9 It is only with reference to specifically *liberal* modernity that this kind of investigation is even worth undertaking. For John Paul II's hostility to the illiberal strands of modernity, such as Nazism and Communism, is too obvious seriously to treat as a question, although an exploration of the grounds of his critique would be a worthwhile enterprise.

10 For a discussion of these and other of the Pope's philosophic influences, see Rocco Buttiglione, *Karol Wojtyła: The Thought of the Man Who Became Pope John Paul II* (Grand Rapids: Wm. B. Eerdmans, 1997).

Chapter 2

1 Although undoubtedly popularized by the 1995 appearance of *Evangelium Vitae*, the term's origins in fact precede the publication of that encyclical. John Paul II used it, for example, during his 1993 visit to the United States. See Alan Cowell, "The Pope in America: Pope Edits His Most Critical Language to End Visit on Positive Note," *The New York Times*, 16 August 1993, sec. A, p. 12. Prior to that he used it in section 39 of his 1991 encyclical *Centesimus Annus* (Boston: St. Paul Books & Media, 1991). Four years

before that the expression had been used in the pope's presence by Chilean Archbishop Jose Manuel Santos Ascarza to describe the "terrorism" of both the state and the opposition in that country. See Roberto Suro, "Pope, in Chile Protest Center, Hears Cry Against Terror," *The New York Times*, 6 April 1987, sec. A, p. 3. Interestingly, the term "culture of death" also appears to have been used by Chilean feminists to express their dissatisfaction with conditions in their country. See Jay Dixon, "Feminist History Conference," *Off Our Backs: A Women's Newsjournal*, 31 July 1986, 1.

2   Perhaps this should not come as a surprise. For, as papal biographer George Weigel has noted, John Paul II himself is both one of the "most visible" and at the same time "least understood" of twentieth century figures. See Weigel, *Witness to Hope*, 4.

3   John Paul II, *Evangelium Vitae* (Boston: St. Paul Books & Media, 1995), sec. 57. All subsequent citations of *Evangelium Vitae* and other papal encyclicals will refer to section, not to page, numbers.

4   *Evangelium Vitae*, 62 and 65.

5   As Weigel notes, although he did not invoke papal infallibility, in condemning the direct and voluntary taking of innocent human life, as well as the specific cases of abortion and euthanasia, John Paul II did appeal to section 25 of *Lumen Gentium*, where the Second Vatican Council "confirmed the infallibility of the 'ordinary, universal Magisterium' of the world's bishops in communion with the Bishop of Rome" (Weigel, *Witness to Hope*, 757). Thus when he addresses the direct taking of innocent human life he invokes "the authority which Christ conferred upon Peter and his Successors" and claims to be speaking "in communion with the Bishops of the Catholic Church." He uses almost identical language in his treatment of abortion, and very similar language in his treatment of euthanasia. The latter, he notes, involves, depending on the situation, the "malice proper" either to murder or suicide, while suicide itself is "always as morally objectionable as murder." See *Evangelium Vitae*, 57, 62, and 65–66.

6   *Evangelium Vitae*, 18.

7   *Evangelium Vitae*, 10.

8   *Evangelium Vitae*, 8 and 18.

9   *Evangelium Vitae*, 4 and 18.

10 Cf. John Paul II's insistence on the traditionally Catholic understanding of Aquinas and Augustine that evil is not itself a positive presence but instead a privation, "the absence of some good which ought to be present in a given being." See his *Memory and Identity* (New York: Rizzoli, 2005), 3–4.

11 *Evangelium Vitae*, 1.

12 *Evangelium Vitae*, 40 and 39.

13 *Evangelium Vitae*, 34.

14 *Evangelium Vitae*, 34.

15 *Evangelium Vitae*, 37.

16 *Evangelium Vitae*, 35. Here he refers to the *Confessions* 1.1. See Augustine, *Confessions*, translated by F. J. Sheed (Indianapolis: Hackett, 1992), 3.

17 *Evangelium Vitae*, 37.

18 *Evangelium Vitae*, 2.

19 *Evangelium Vitae*, 38. Cf. the *Catechism of the Catholic Church*, 2nd ed. (Libreria Editrice Vaticana, 1997), sec. 27 (quoting *Gaudium et Spes*): "The dignity of man rests above all on the fact that he is called to communion with God."

20 *Evangelium Vitae*, 52.

21 *Veritatis Splendor* (Boston: Pauline Books & Media, 1993), secs. 12, 13, and 39. For a similar discussion of the issues in this section, consider John Paul II, *Memory and Identity*, 27–30.

22 *Evangelium Vitae*, 75 and 3.

23 Cf. *Memory and Identity*, 35, where John Paul II indicates that for the "Aristotelian-Thomistic tradition" the "accomplishment of a just good is always accompanied by an interior joy—the joy of the good."

24 *Veritatis Splendor*, 41.

25 *Evangelium Vitae*, 48.

26 *Veritatis Splendor*, 7.

27 *Veritatis Splendor*, 72. Cf. *Familiaris Consortio*, where the Pope insists on the "primacy of moral values, which are the values of the human person as such" and therefore are bound up with "the ultimate meaning of life." He continues later: "Since the moral order reveals and sets forth the plan of God the Creator, for this very reason it cannot be something that harms man, something impersonal. On the contrary, by responding to the deepest demands of the human being created by God, it places itself at the service of that person's full humanity with the delicate and binding love whereby God Himself inspires, sustains and guides every creature towards its happiness" (*Familiaris Consortio* [Boston: Pauline Books & Media, 1981], secs. 8 and 34).

28 *Familiaris Consortio*, 8 and 34.

29 *Evangelium Vitae*, 75.

30 *Evangelium Vitae*, 41 and 40.

31 *Evangelium Vitae*, 25 and 2.

32 See Mark 8:35 and Luke 9:24. This paradox, John Paul suggests in *Laborem Exercens*, can be experienced even in our most ordinary daily activities. Work, he notes, inevitably involves an element of toil. "And yet in spite of all this toil—perhaps, in a sense, because of it—work is a good thing for man. Even though it bears the mark of a *bonum arduum*, in the terminology of St. Thomas, this does not take away the fact that, as such, it is a good thing for man," for it "corresponds to" and "expresses" his "dignity" and allows man to achieve "fulfillment as a human being" and to become "more a human being" (*Laborem Exercens* [Boston: Pauline Books & Media, 1981], sec. 9).

33 *Evangelium Vitae*, 49.

34 *Familiaris Consortio*, 11 (emphases in original).

35 *Evangelium Vitae*, 1.

36 *Evangelium Vitae*, 77 (emphases added).

37 *Evangelium Vitae*, 40 and 100.

38 *Evangelium Vitae*, 77.

39 *Evangelium Vitae*, 24.

40 *Evangelium Vitae*, 2.

41 *Centesimus Annus*, 24. Cf. John Paul II, *Memory and Identity*, 152: "The question about man, which is asked repeatedly, finds its complete answer in Jesus Christ." Also, see *Fides et Ratio* (Boston: Pauline Books & Media, 1998), sec. 12, in which the Holy Father contends that "the mystery of personal existence," with its questions posed by "pain, the suffering of the innocent and death," remains "an insoluble riddle" when viewed in any terms other than those of "the mystery of the incarnate Word."

42 *Fides et Ratio*, 32.

43 *Evangelium Vitae*, 81.

44 This is not to say, of course, that the Pope would hold that man can, through his own moral effort alone, achieve this union with God. The role of grace in man's achievement of the supreme good is, however, beyond the scope of the present argument.

45 *Evangelium Vitae*, 27 and 5.

46 *Evangelium Vitae*, 63.

47 *Evangelium Vitae*, 67.

48 *Evangelium Vitae*, 54.

49 *Evangelium Vitae*, 19 and 8.

50 *Evangelium Vitae*, 21.

51 *Evangelium Vitae*, 21 and 22.

52   The argument of the encyclical thus seems in harmony with that of Romans
     1:18-32. St. Paul argues there, after all, that when human beings turn from
     God they are led to embrace "dishonorable" passions and conduct. That is,
     the loss of God leads to a loss of the sense of the dignity of human nature,
     and hence to "all manner of wickedness."
53   *Veritatis Splendor*, 106 and 32.
54   *Evangelium Vitae*, 19.
55   *Evangelium Vitae*, 48.
56   *Veritatis Splendor*, 18.
57   *Evangelium Vitae*, 23.
58   *Evangelium Vitae*, 23, 64, and 12.
59   *Evangelium Vitae*, 10, 59, and 18.
60   *Evangelium Vitae*, 20.
61   *Sollicitudo Rei Socialis* (Boston: Pauline Books & Media, 1987), sec. 28.
62   Quoted in *Sollicitudo Rei Socialis*, 10. See James 4:1-2.
63   *Evangelium Vitae*, 20.
64   *Evangelium Vitae*, 70.
65   *Evangelium Vitae*, 20, 70, and 20.
66   *Letter to Families*, 21.
67   *Evangelium Vitae*, 20.
68   *Evangelium Vitae*, 20.
69   *Evangelium Vitae*, 70.
70   *Centesimus Annus*, 47.
71   *Veritatis Splendor*, 101.
72   *Veritatis Splendor*, 99.
73   *Evangelium Vitae*, 71.
74   *Evangelium Vitae*, 18.
75   *Evangelium Vitae*, 64.
76   *Evangelium Vitae*, 36.
77   *Evangelium Vitae*, 19.
78   *Evangelium Vitae*, 41 and 42.
79   *Evangelium Vitae*, 18.
80   *Sollicitudo Rei Socialis*, 92.

Chapter 3

1   *Evangelium Vitae*, 2.
2   Thomas Hobbes, *Leviathan*, edited by Richard Tuck (New York: Cambridge
    University Press, 1991), 9 (emphases in original). In this chapter I quote

from Hobbes's text without modification, and so leave untouched the *Leviathan*'s archaic spelling, punctuation, capitalization, grammar, and frequent use of italicization. Unless otherwise indicated, emphases are Hobbes's.

3   Hobbes, *Leviathan*, 151.

4   Hobbes, *Leviathan*, 9.

5   *Evangelium Vitae*, 34.

6   Hobbes, *Leviathan*, 9 and 26.

7   Hobbes, *Leviathan*, 32 and 21.

8   Hobbes, *Leviathan*, 22–23.

9   John Paul II, *Memory and Identity*, 35 and 39–40.

10 See book 6 of the *Nicomachean Ethics* and book 1, chapter 2 of the *Politics*.

11 Hobbes, *Leviathan*, 119–20.

12 Hobbes, *Leviathan*, 34.

13 Hobbes, *Leviathan*, 58–59.

14 Hobbes, *Leviathan*, 146–47.

15 Hobbes, *Leviathan*, 44.

16 Consider *Veritatis Splendor*, 42: "Patterned on God's freedom, man's freedom is not negated by his obedience to the divine law; indeed, only through this obedience does it abide in the truth and conform to human dignity. This is clearly stated by the Council: 'Human dignity requires man to act through conscious and free choice, as motivated and prompted personally from within, and not through blind internal impulse or merely external pressure. Man achieves such dignity when he frees himself from all subservience to his feelings, and in a free choice of the good, pursues his own end by effectively and assiduously marshalling the appropriate means."

17 Hobbes, *Leviathan*, 144.

18 Man's natural sociability is expressly affirmed in section 12 of *Gaudium et Spes*, the Second Vatican Council's "Pastoral Constitution on the Church in the Modern World," to which John Paul II refers frequently in his social encyclicals. See Austin Flannery, O.P., general editor, *Vatican Council II*, vol. 1: *The Conciliar and Post Conciliar Documents* (Northport, N.Y.: Costello Publishing, 1998), 913.

19 Hobbes, *Leviathan*, 99.

20 Hobbes, *Leviathan*, 83.

21 Hobbes, *Leviathan*, 75. Notice that even here Hobbes leaves open the possibility that man's natural religiosity arises not from a qualitative difference from other animals but from a mere difference of degree.

22 Quoted in *Evangelium Vitae*, 35.
23 Hobbes, *Leviathan*, 70.
24 Hobbes, *Leviathan*, 76.
25 Hobbes, *Leviathan*, 77.
26 Hobbes, *Leviathan*, 87–89.
27 Hobbes, *Leviathan*, 87.
28 Hobbes, *Leviathan*, 92.
29 Hobbes, *Leviathan*, 90.
30 Hobbes, *Leviathan*, 100.
31 Hobbes, *Leviathan*, 89.
32 Hobbes, *Leviathan*, 90.
33 Hobbes, *Leviathan*, 39 and 31.
34 Hobbes, *Leviathan*, 111 and 53.
35 Hobbes, *Leviathan*, 133 and 176.
36 Hobbes, *Leviathan*, 236.
37 Hobbes, *Leviathan*, 99.
38 Hobbes, *Leviathan*, 90 and 88.
39 Hobbes, *Leviathan*, 106–10.
40 Hobbes, *Leviathan*, 91.
41 Hobbes, *Leviathan*, 109.
42 Hobbes, *Leviathan*, 94.
43 Hobbes, *Leviathan*, 202.
44 Hobbes, *Leviathan*, 111.
45 Hobbes, *Leviathan*, 103.
46 See Plato's *Republic*, translated by Allan Bloom (New York: Basic Books, 1968), 36.
47 Hobbes, *Leviathan*, 117.
48 Hobbes, *Leviathan*, 204.
49 Hobbes, *Leviathan*, 204. See also Plato's *Republic*, 37.
50 Hobbes, *Leviathan*, 101.
51 Consider especially chapter 15, "Of Those Things for which Men, and Especially Princes, are Praised or Blamed," and chapter 18, "In what Mode Princes Ought to Keep Faith," in *The Prince*, translated by Leo Paul S. de Alvarez (Prospect Heights, Ill.: Waveland Press, 1980).
52 Hobbes, *Leviathan*, 102–3.
53 Hobbes, *Leviathan*, 91.
54 Hobbes, *Leviathan*, 53.
55 Hobbes, *Leviathan*, 54 and 93.
56 Hobbes, *Leviathan*, 87.

57 Hobbes, *Leviathan*, 142 and 235.

58 Hobbes, *Leviathan*, 163.

59 It is on the basis of such an argument that some contemporary Darwinian political and moral theorists suggest that infanticide is immoral. See my discussion of such thinkers in *The Right Darwin: Evolution, Religion, and the Future of Democracy* (Dallas: Spence Publishing, 2006), 34–35.

60 Hobbes, *Leviathan*, 89, 41, and 140.

61 Hobbes, *Leviathan*, 235–36.

62 Hobbes, *Leviathan*, 140.

63 Hobbes, *Leviathan*, 62–63.

64 Hobbes, *Leviathan*, 239, 125, and 130.

65 Hobbes, *Leviathan*, 132.

66 Hobbes, *Leviathan*, 124.

67 Hobbes, *Leviathan*, 219.

68 Hobbes, *Leviathan*, 219.

69 Hobbes, *Leviathan*, 122.

70 Hobbes, *Leviathan*, 124.

71 Hobbes, *Leviathan*, 148. It is true that Hobbes holds that it is against the law of nature to punish the innocent. His point here, however, is a legal one. He refers not to the morally innocent but to the legally innocent, those who have been judicially acquitted of a crime and yet are punished for having fled when first accused, on the legal presumption that flight demonstrates guilt. Hobbes makes clear that he could support such punishment if it were based on a written law forbidding flight rather than a legal presupposition. See 192–93.

72 Hobbes, *Leviathan*, 148 and 221.

73 Hobbes, *Leviathan*, 3.

74 See Aubrey's *Life of Hobbes*, reproduced in the front matter of the edition of *Leviathan* edited by Edwin Curley (Indianapolis: Hackett, 1994), lxvii; and Sir Leslie Stephen's *Hobbes* (Ann Arbor: University of Michigan Press, 1961), 150.

75 Hobbes, *Leviathan*, 229, 372 and 260.

76 Hobbes, *Leviathan*, 248 and 111.

77 Hobbes, *Leviathan*, 74–75.

78 Hobbes, *Leviathan*, 252 and 250.

Chapter 4

1 John Locke, *Second Treatise of Civil Government*, in *Two Treatises of Government*, edited by Peter Laslett (New York: New American Library,

1963), sec. 4. Here and in subsequent references to the treatises I refer not to the page numbers of the Laslett edition but to Locke's section numbers. In this chapter I quote from Locke's text without modification, and so leave untouched his archaic spelling, punctuation, capitalization, grammar, and frequent use of italicization. Unless otherwise noted, emphases are his.

2 Locke, *Second Treatise*, 4 (emphasis added).

3 Locke, *Second Treatise*, 6.

4 Locke, *Second Treatise*, 6.

5 Locke, *Second Treatise*, 14.

6 Locke, *Second Treatise*, 195.

7 Locke, *Second Treatise*, 135.

8 Locke, *Second Treatise*, 135.

9 Locke, *Second Treatise*, 199.

10 Locke, *Second Treatise*, 201.

11 Locke, *Second Treatise*, 65 and 170.

12 Locke, *First Treatise*, 52.

13 Locke, *First Treatise*, 56.

14 Locke, *First Treatise*, 89. See also *Second Treatise*, 66 and 78–79.

15 Locke, *Second Treatise*, 67.

16 Locke, *Second Treatise*, 6.

17 Locke, *First Treatise*, 42.

18 Locke, *Second Treatise*, 183.

19 Those familiar with the work of Leo Strauss will discern that my reading of the *Two Treatises* has been influenced by his account of Locke in *Natural Right and History* (Chicago: University of Chicago Press, 1953).

20 In contrast to the argument offered here, some scholars—such as Nathan Tarcov in *Locke's Education for Liberty* (Chicago: University of Chicago Press, 1984)—downplay Locke's supposed individualism, while others— such as Jeremy Waldron in *God, Locke, and Equality: Christian Foundations of John Locke's Political Thought* (New York: Cambridge University Press, 2002)—present him as a Christian thinker. My argument does not deny the aspects of Locke's teaching that such scholars emphasize. It does suggest, however, that from the standpoint of *Evangelium Vitae*'s argument, at least some aspects of Locke's teaching tend to erode its ability to sustain a proper respect for human dignity and human rights.

21 Locke, *Second Treatise*, 101. See also 77.

22 Locke, *Second Treatise*, 123–25.

23 Locke, *Second Treatise*, 20.

24 Consider *Second Treatise*, 6, where Locke says that "Every one" is "bound to preserve himself," and 168, where he says that it is "out of a Man's power so to submit himself to another, as to give him a liberty to destroy him; God and Nature never allowing a Man so to abandon himself, as to neglect his own preservation." These statements, by including all men, necessarily include even the unjust aggressor, whose life will indeed be in danger from the man he has tried to victimize.

25 Locke, *Second Treatise*, 7.

26 Locke, *Second Treatise*, 136.

27 Locke, *Second Treatise* 127, and Hobbes, *Leviathan*, 90.

28 Locke, *Second Treatise*, 127.

29 Locke, *Second Treatise*, 134 and 131.

30 Locke, *Second Treatise*, 6.

31 Locke, *Second Treatise*, 149.

32 Locke, *Second Treatise*, 26.

33 Locke, *Second Treatise*, 6.

34 Locke, *First Treatise*, 87 and 92.

35 Locke, *Second Treatise*, 26. See also 34. In this connection consider Richard Kennington's similar observation that Locke is a Hobbesian hedonist for whom morality is subordinated to the quest for pleasure. See his *On Modern Origins: Essays in Early Modern Philosophy*, edited by Pamela Kraus and Frank Hunt (Lanham, Md.: Lexington Books, 2004), 258 and 260.

36 Locke, *Second Treatise*, 94, 134, and 149.

37 Locke, *Second Treatise*, 11, 172, 181.

38 See *Evangelium Vitae*, 56.

39 Locke, *Second Treatise*, 172.

40 Locke, *Second Treatise*, 11.

41 Genesis 4:15, in *The New Oxford Annotated Bible*, edited by Herbert G. May and Bruce M. Metzger (New York: Oxford University Press, 1962) [RSV].

42 Locke, *Second Treatise*, 23.

43 Locke, *Second Treatise*, 23 and 6.

44 Locke, *First Treatise*, 88.

45 For a different view, see Gary D. Glenn, "Inalienable Rights and Locke's Argument for Limited Government: Political Implications of a Right to Suicide," *Journal of Politics* 46.1 (1984): 80–105.

46 Locke, *First Treatise*, 88.

47 It must be admitted, however, that in Locke's teaching children at least enjoy a better position than in that of Hobbes. Locke ranks care for

offspring as the second most powerful human passion, while for Hobbes, as we have seen in chapter 3, it is not even among the top three.

48 See *Veritatis Splendor*, 90–94.

49 Locke, *Second Treatise*, 149.

50 Locke, *Second Treatise*, 209.

51 The argument advanced in this paragraph is similar to the account of Lockeanism's openness to slavery offered by Harry Jaffa in *Crisis of the House Divided* (Seattle: University of Washington Press, 1959), 322–29, and Herbert Storing in *Toward a More Perfect Union*, edited by Joseph M. Bessette (Washington: The AEI Press, 1995), 142–44.

Chapter 5

1 David Hume, *An Enquiry Concerning the Principles of Morals*, edited by Tom L. Beauchamp (Oxford: Oxford University Press, 1998), 6–7. Unless otherwise indicated, in all subsequent references I have abbreviated this entry as *Enquiry*.

2 Niccolo Machiavelli, *The Prince*, translated by Leo Paul S. de Alvarez (Prospect Heights, Ill.: Waveland Press, 1980), 93.

3 *Enquiry*, 108–9. As with Hobbes and Locke, I have made no modernizations of Hume's English.

4 David Hume, *A Treatise of Human Nature*, edited by David Fate Norton and Mary J. Norton (Oxford: Oxford University Press, 2000), 261–62.

5 Hume, *Treatise*, 266.

6 *Enquiry*, 85–86.

7 Hume, *Treatise*, 363–64. See Robert S. Hill's suggestion that Hume is "following the line laid down by Hobbes and Locke in trying to erect morals" on a basis that the passions can approve with a view to making "the obligatory *effectively* obligatory" ("David Hume," in *History of Political Philosophy*, edited by Leo Strauss and Joseph Cropsey, 3rd ed. [Chicago: University of Chicago Press, 1987], 542–43 [emphasis in original]).

8 *Enquiry*, 3.

9 *Enquiry*, 34 and 5–6. Hume also suggests that when we speak the language of morality we seek to "move some universal principle of the human frame, and touch a string, to which all mankind have an accord and symphony" (75).

10 *Enquiry*, 91 and 35.

11 *Enquiry*, 35.

12 *Enquiry*, 37.

13 *Enquiry Concerning Human Understanding*, edited by Tom L. Beauchamp (Oxford: Clarendon, 2000), 7.

14 Hume, *Treatise*, 368.

15 *Enquiry*, 39.

16 *Enquiry*, 42, 44–45. See also Hume, *Treatise*, 394.

17 Hobbes, *Leviathan*, 111.

18 *Enquiry*, 34 and 89.

19 *Enquiry*, 43 (emphasis added).

20 *Enquiry*, 94. See also 81, where Hume contends that, because the "goods of fortune" must be "spent in one gratification or another," it would "be difficult to show, why a man is more a loser by a generous action" than its opposite, since he thereby gratifies his benevolence where the miser would have gratified his "avarice." This argument is intended, of course, as a defense of generosity, but it can go no further than to show that generosity is just as natural as avarice, not that it is more natural than avarice.

21 *Enquiry*, 44.

22 Thus Humean sympathy is like Locke's law of nature. Both turn out to be quibbles with Hobbes that do not prevent Hume's and Locke's teachings from being *practically* Hobbesian.

23 *Enquiry*, 73.

24 *Enquiry*, 47–48 and 56.

25 In this connection we might also consider Hume's contention that the ultimate reason for all human conduct is to avoid pain and enjoy pleasure. See *Enquiry*, 88–89.

26 *Enquiry*, 51–52. The way that Hume's hedonistic sociability influences his judgments of human worth can also be seen in the following remark: "What derision and contempt, with both sexes, attend impotence; while the unhappy object is regarded as one deprived of so capital a pleasure in life, and at the same time, as disabled from communicating it to others" (*Enquiry*, 55).

27 *Evangelium Vitae*, 12.

28 *Enquiry*, 15.

29 *Enquiry*, 16.

30 *Enquiry*, 16.

31 Hume also suggests that in such situations individuals may likewise act to preserve society if the government fails to do so. Thus he indicates that we would not regard it as "criminal or injurious" if, in a "famine," any "number of men" were "to assemble, without the tye of laws or civil jurisdiction," and enforce, "by power and even violence," an "equal partition of bread" (*Enquiry*, 15).

32 *Enquiry*, 15.
33 *Enquiry*, 15 (emphasis added).
34 *Enquiry*, 15–16.
35 *Enquiry*, 79
36 *Enquiry*, 81.
37 *Enquiry*, 81.
38 *Enquiry*, 81–82.
39 *Enquiry*, 82.
40 *Enquiry*, 82.
41 *Enquiry*, 6–7.
42 *Enquiry*, 73. Hume also says that some supposed virtues are in fact "austere pretenders" that should be dismissed as "hypocrites or deceivers," or at most considered the "least favoured" of the virtues (80).
43 Hume, *Treatise*, 6 and 311.
44 Locke, *Second Treatise*, 123.
45 *Enquiry*, 28.
46 This is not, by the way, the only time that Hume implicitly draws upon moral resources that are in fact alien to his teaching. In the second section of the *Enquiry*, titled "Of Benevolence," he remarks, uncontroversially, that "the benevolent or softer affections"—affections indicated by such terms as *"sociable, good-natured, humane, merciful, grateful, friendly, generous, beneficent"*—"are ESTIMABLE," that "wherever they appear" they "engage the approbation, and good-will of mankind." He then ventures onto much thinner ice, however, by adding that not only are such terms or "their equivalents" known "to all languages," but also "universally express the highest merit, which *human nature* is capable of attaining" (*Enquiry*, 8). It requires only a passing familiarity with ancient Sparta or Rome, or any other warrior culture, to recognize that "the benevolent or softer affections" have not been accorded the "highest merit" in all human societies. Thus Shakespeare could depict the republican Romans as accepting Coriolanus—a man notorious for his deficiencies in the "benevolent or softer affections"—as the most virtuous citizen, precisely because not benevolence but "valour" was "held" to be "the chiefest virtue" that "[m]ost dignifies the haver" (*Coriolanus*, edited by Philip Brockbank [New York: Routledge, 1976], 173). Because the benevolent passions are so important to his moral teaching, Hume exaggerates their prominence in human nature, contrary to the evidence that experience actually provides. Thus he seeks to enhance their natural authority in order to avoid having

to appeal to Christian morality, the influence of which arguably informs his exaltation of benevolence.

47 Hobbes, *Leviathan*, 99.

48 Machiavelli, *The Prince*, 109.

49 Consider the division in American public opinion provoked by the tragic case of Terri Schiavo. Some Americans sympathized more with her and her family, and some more with her husband.

50 *Enquiry*, 44, 98, and 41.

51 *Enquiry*, 18. I am indebted to Larry Arnhart for first calling this passage to my attention. See his *Darwinian Natural Right: The Biological Ethics of Human Nature* (Albany: State University of New York Press, 1998), 180.

52 Inasmuch as Hume holds that justice itself depends on sympathy or humanity, we might wonder how this can be. That is, if justice depends on our sympathetic concern for others, how can we speak of the latter as still exerting influence on our actions where justice has no place? Hume is not involved in self-contradiction, however. He holds that justice as a scheme of rules and rights depends on our sympathetic concern for society, which is generally well served by justice. Here, however, he suggests that when justice is no longer generally useful, and therefore no longer engages our sympathy for society in general, we still might feel sympathy for the particular persons who are no longer protected by justice.

53 *Enquiry*, 18.

Chapter 6

1 See Philip B. Kurland and Ralph Lerner, eds., *The Founders' Constitution*, vol. 1: *Major Themes* (Chicago: University of Chicago Press, 1987), 9.

2 See the view put forward by Stephen Douglas in Paul M. Angle, ed., *The Complete Lincoln-Douglas Debates of 1858* (Chicago: University of Chicago Press, 1991), 200–1. Consider also Chief Justice Roger Taney's similar understanding, expressed in his opinion for the Supreme Court in *Dred Scott v. Sandford* (1857), which is excerpted in Ralph A. Rossum and G. Alan Tarr's *American Constitutional Law*, vol. 1: *The Structure of Government*, 5th ed. (New York: St. Martin's/Worth, 1999), 271–80.

3 Kurland and Lerner, *The Founders' Constitution*, 11.

4 Quoted in Walter Isaacson, *Benjamin Franklin: An American Life* (New York: Simon & Schuster, 2003), 313.

5 Kurland and Lerner, *The Founders' Constitution*, 10.

6 Kurland and Lerner, *The Founders' Constitution*, 9 and 10–11.

7   Quoted in *American Political Rhetoric*, edited by Peter Augustine Lawler and Robert Martin Schaefer, 4th ed. (Lanham, Md.: Rowman & Littlefield, 2001), 236. Similar implications must have been present to Jefferson's mind even at the time the *Declaration* was drafted. The initial draft contained a reference to the slave trade which was omitted from the final version.

8   *Veritatis Splendor*, 41.

9   *The Republic of Plato*, translated by Allan Bloom (New York: Basic Books, 1968), 41 and 42–43. Note the similarity between Socrates' response to Glaucon and Adeimantus' account of justice and John Paul II's response to the culture of death.

10 *The Works of James Wilson*, edited by Robert Green McCloskey, vol. 2 (Cambridge, Mass.: The Belknap Press of Harvard University Press, 1967), 596–97. Wilson's account suggests that these practices were informed by a utilitarian understanding of human life similar to that criticized by John Paul II. Thus it was that, among the Spartans, children who appeared "ill formed or unhealthy" were "thrown into a gulph near mount Taygetus."

11 *The Papers of James Madison*, edited by Robert A. Rutland, vol. 9 (Chicago: University of Chicago Press), 141. One might also consider in this connection Madison's well-known argument in the *Tenth Federalist* that a majority can itself be a faction committed to unjust policy.

12 Thomas Jefferson, *Writings*, edited Merrill D. Peterson (New York: Library of America, 1984), 1501.

13 Alexander Hamilton, *Selected Writings and Speeches of Alexander Hamilton*, edited by Morton J. Frisch (Washington: American Enterprise Institute for Public Policy Research, 1985), 19–22.

14 John Adams, *The Revolutionary Writings of John Adams*, edited by C. Bradley Thompson (Indianapolis: Liberty Fund, 2001), 33.

15 Adams, *Revolutionary Writings*, 287–88.

16 *George Washington: A Collection*, edited by William B. Allen (Indianapolis: Liberty Fund, 1988), 249.

17 See *Political Sermons of the Founding Era*, vol. 1, edited by Ellis Sandoz (Indianapolis: Liberty Fund, 1998), 909–40.

18 Adams, *Revolutionary Writings*, 287.

19 Adams, *Revolutionary Writings*, 297. See also article VII, which offers a somewhat reductive definition of the "common good" as the "protection, safety, prosperity, and happiness of the people" (299).

20 Jefferson, *Writings*, 424.

21 Jefferson, *Writings*, 423.

22 As Alan Gibson's recent study shows, the study of American political thought over the last century has primarily been an argument among partisans of different interpretations. This contest has in turn led some scholars to suggest a "multiple traditions" approach to understanding the founding, a turn that might be understood as implying the Founding's fundamental theoretical ambiguity. See Alan Gibson, *Interpreting the Founding: Guide to the Enduring Debates Over the Origins and Foundations of the American Republic* (Lawrence: University of Kansas Press, 2006).

23 Consider, for example, his remarks upon receiving Lindy Boggs, American Ambassador to the Holy See, in 1997, which are reprinted as "John Paul II on the American Experiment," *First Things* 82 (1998): 36–37.

24 See sections 44 (where he speaks of America as a continent "marked by . . . unbridled consumerism"), 56 (where he notes the prevalence of a "neoliberalism" that rests on a "purely economic conception of man" that "considers profit and the law of the market as its only parameters, to the detriment of the dignity of and the respect due to individuals and peoples"), and especially 63 (where he contends that today "in America as elsewhere in the world, a model of society appears to be emerging in which the powerful predominate, setting aside and even eliminating the powerless"). See *Ecclesia in America*, Vatican Website, http://www.vatican.va/holy_father/john_paul_ii/apost_exhortations/documents/hf_jp-ii_exh_22011999_ecclesia-in-america_en.html (accessed 1 June 2007).

Chapter 7

1 Alexis de Tocqueville, *Democracy in America*, translated by Harvey Mansfield and Delba Winthrop (Chicago: University of Chicago Press, 2000), 3, 52, 479–82.

2 Tocqueville, *Democracy in America*, 4 and 6.

3 Tocqueville, *Democracy in America*, 413. Tocqueville even goes so far as to identify the modern progress of equality with God's will. It is, he suggests, a "providential fact" (6–7).

4 Tocqueville, *Democracy in America*, 676.

5 Tocqueville, *Democracy in America*, 417–18.

6 Tocqueville, *Democracy in America*, 299.

7 Tocqueville, *Democracy in America*, 424.

8 Tocqueville, *Democracy in America*, 403–4. Tocqueville's account of how democracy erodes the credibility of belief in God, by the way, is compatible with the earnestness about religion that could still be observed in the

Americans of his day. The Americans, he contends, are acutely aware of the contribution made by religion to the preservation of their republican freedom. On close observation, he adds, "one will see that religion itself reigns there" not so much as "revealed doctrine" but as one of the "ready-made opinions" supplied by the majority (409).

9   Tocqueville, *Democracy in America*, 452 and 454.

10   Tocqueville, *Democracy in America*, 412–13.

11   Tocqueville, *Democracy in America*, 425–26.

12   Tocqueville, *Democracy in America*, 426.

13   Tocqueville, *Democracy in America*, 483.

14   Tocqueville, *Democracy in America*, 483–84. Also, see Tocqueville's primary account of the importance of laws of inheritance and how the democratic and aristocratic variants influence the character of the family (46–52).

15   Tocqueville, *Democracy in America*, 482–83.

16   Tocqueville, *Democracy in America*, 506.

17   Tocqueville, *Democracy in America*, 506–7.

18   Tocqueville, *Democracy in America*, 507–8.

19   Tocqueville, *Democracy in America*, 509.

20   Tocqueville, *Democracy in America*, 414.

21   Tocqueville, *Democracy in America*, 663.

22   Tocqueville, *Democracy in America*, 500–1.

23   Tocqueville, *Democracy in America*, 500–1 and 506.

24   Tocqueville, *Democracy in America*, 227–28.

25   Tocqueville, *Democracy in America*, 535–37.

26   Tocqueville, *Democracy in America*, 538.

27   Tocqueville, *Democracy in America*, 535 and 538.

28   Tocqueville, *Democracy in America*, 545.

29   Tocqueville, *Democracy in America*, 538 and 303.

30   Tocqueville, *Democracy in America*, 485–86.

31   Tocqueville, *Democracy in America*, 515–16.

32   See the *Politics* 1253b23–1255b15 and 1278b6–1279b10.

33   John Stuart Mill, *On Liberty* (Indianapolis: Hackett, 1978), 9–10.

34   We might also observe in passing that the distinction between despotism and tyranny is relevant to the proper treatment of some of the kinds of people that John Paul II views as being primarily threatened by the culture of death. For example, unborn children, the comatose, as well as certain gravely disabled adults would have to be ruled despotically, since by the nature of their situations they cannot contribute to deci-

sions that affect them, but should not be ruled tyrannically, since they remain human beings with rights that ought not be subordinated to other people's interests.

35 Tocqueville, *Democracy in America*, 516.
36 See *Democracy in America*, 275, for Tocqueville's explanation of his use of the term *mores*.
37 Tocqueville, *Democracy in America*, 240.
38 Tocqueville, *Democracy in America*, 409 and 641.
39 Tocqueville, *Democracy in America*, 236.
40 Tocqueville, *Democracy in America*, 237. See also 243–45.

Chapter 8

1   *Memory and Identity*, 3–4.
2   *Memory and Identity*, 7–8.
3   *Memory and Identity*, 97. See also where John Paul II speaks of an "openness toward Christ, which the Enlightenment excluded" (116).
4   *Memory and Identity*, 99.
5   *Memory and Identity*, 7–8.
6   *Memory and Identity*, 9–11.
7   John Paul II offers a similar account of modernity's philosophic inclinations and their moral consequences in section 5 of *Fides et Ratio*. There he contends that the "reason" of modern philosophy, "in its one sided concern to investigate human subjectivity, seems to have forgotten that men and women are always called to direct their steps toward a truth which transcends them." He concludes that, apart from that truth, "individuals are at the mercy of caprice, and their state as persons ends up being judged by pragmatic criteria based essentially on experimental data, in the mistaken belief that technology must dominate all."
8   *Memory and Identity*, 34–35.
9   *Memory and Identity*, 11.
10 *Memory and Identity*, 12.
11 Tocqueville, *Democracy in America*, 400.
12 For a discussion of Wojtyła's role in the preparation of *Gaudium et Spes* see Weigel's *Witness to Hope*, 166–69.
13 *Memory and Identity*, 109–10. See then-Cardinal Ratzinger's similar remark in his exchange with Marcello Pera, *Without Roots: The West, Relativism, Christianity, Islam* (New York: Basic Books, 2006), 116.
14 Tocqueville, *Democracy in America*, 460.

15 Tocqueville, *Democracy in America*, 675.

16 *Memory and Identity*, 3–4.

17 *Memory and Identity*, 98.

18 *Fides et Ratio*, 5.

19 *Memory and Identity*, 98.

20 *Memory and Identity*, 107–8.

21 *Memory and Identity*, 109.

22 Tocqueville, *Democracy in America*, 412–13.

23 *The Elements of Law*, edited by Ferdinand Tönnies, 2nd ed. (London: Frank Cass, 1969), xv.

24 Tocqueville, *Democracy in America*, 419. See also 504–6 and 517–21.

25 Tocqueville, *Democracy in America*, 279–80.

26 Tocqueville, *Democracy in America*, 431. See also 283–84, 287, and 510–11.

27 Compare Tocqueville's *Democracy in America*, 510–11 and 517.

28 Tocqueville, *Democracy in America*, 504–5.

29 Tocqueville, *Democracy in America*, 502. Tocqueville indicates that one sometimes sees Americans giving way to such inclinations. Thus even under democratic conditions the nobler parts of human nature can assert themselves, despite the public elevation of a morality based on enlightened self-interest.

30 Tocqueville, *Democracy in America*, 519.

31 Tocqueville, *Democracy in America*.

32 John 15:13 [RSV].

33 Psalms 8:4-5 [RSV].

34 See Nietzsche's *Beyond Good and Evil: Prelude to a Philosophy of the Future*, translated by Walter Kaufmann (New York: Vintage Books, 1966), sec. 260 (pp. 204–8).

BIBLIOGRAPHY

Adams, John. 2001. *The Revolutionary Writings of John Adams*. Edited by
  C. Bradley Thompson. Indianapolis: Liberty Fund, 2001.

Angle, Paul M., ed. 1991. *The Complete Lincoln-Douglas Debates of 1858*.
  Chicago: University of Chicago Press.

Aristotle. 1999. *Nicomachean Ethics*. Translated by H. Rackham. Cambridge, Mass.: Harvard University Press.

———. 1984. *Politics*. Translated by Carnes Lord. Chicago: University
  of Chicago Press.

Arnhart, Larry. 1998. *Darwinian Natural Right: The Biological Ethics of
  Human Nature*. Albany: State University of New York Press.

Augustine. 1992. *Confessions*. Translated by F. J. Sheed. Indianapolis:
  Hackett.

Bernstein, Carl, and Marco Politi. 1996. *His Holiness: John Paul II and the
  Hidden History of Our Time*. New York: Doubleday.

Bottum, Joseph. 2005. "John Paul the Great: 1920–2005." *Weekly
  Standard*, 18 April: 20–30.

Boyle, Peter J. 2005. "A Hard Faith." *New Yorker*, 16 May: 54–65.

Buttiglione, Rocco. 1997. *Karol Wojtyła: The Thought of the Man Who
  Became Pope John Paul II*. Grand Rapid: Eerdmans.

Catechism of the Catholic Church. 1997. 2nd ed. Libreria Editrice Vaticana.

Cowell, Alan. 1993. "The Pope in America: Pope Edits His Most Critical Language to End Visit on Positive Note." The New York Times, 16 August: sec. A, p. 12.

Currie, Duncan. 2005. "Misunderstanding John Paul II." Weekly Standard, 18 April: 15–16.

Dixon, Jay. 1986. "Feminist History Conference." Off Our Backs: A Women's Newsjournal, 31 July: 1.

Flannery, Austin, O.P., ed. 1998. Vatican Council II. Vol. 1: The Conciliar and Post Conciliar Documents. Northport, N.Y.: Costello Publishing.

Gibson, Alan. 2006. Interpreting the Founding: Guide to the Enduring Debates over the Origins and Foundations of the American Republic. Lawrence: University Press of Kansas.

Glenn, Gary D. 1984. "Inalienable Rights and Locke's Argument for Limited Government: Political Implications of a Right to Suicide. Journal of Politics 46, no. 1: 80–105.

Hamilton, Alexander. 1985. Selected Writings and Speeches of Alexander Hamilton. Edited by Morton J. Frisch. Washington: American Enterprise Institute for Public Policy Research.

Hill, Robert S. 1987. "David Hume." In History of Political Philosophy. Edited by Leo Strauss and Joseph Cropsey. 3rd ed. Chicago: University of Chicago Press, 535–58.

Hobbes, Thomas. 1994. Leviathan. Edited by Edwin Curley. Indianapolis: Hackett.

———. 1991. Leviathan. Edited by Richard Tuck. New York: Cambridge University Press.

———. 1969. The Elements of Law. Edited by Ferdinand Tönnies. 2nd ed. London: Frank Cass.

Holloway, Carson. 2006. The Right Darwin: Evolution, Religion, and the Future of Democracy. Dallas: Spence Publishing.

Hume, David. 2000. A Treatise of Human Nature. Edited by David Fate Norton and Mary J. Norton. Oxford: Oxford University Press.

———. 2000. An Enquiry Concerning Human Understanding. Edited by Tom L. Beauchamp. Oxford: Clarendon.

———. 1998. *An Enquiry Concerning the Principles of Morals.* Edited by Tom L. Beauchamp. Oxford: Oxford University Press.

Isaacson, Walter. 2003. *Benjamin Franklin: An American Life.* New York: Simon & Schuster.

Jaffa, Harry V. 1959. *Crisis of the House Divided.* Seattle: University of Washington Press.

Jefferson, Thomas. 1984. *Writings.* Edited by Merrill D. Peterson. New York: Library of America.

John Paul II. 2005. *Memory and Identity: Conversations at the Dawn of a Millennium.* New York: Rizzoli International.

———. 1999. *Ecclesia in America.* Vatican Website: http://www.vatican.va/holy_father/john_paul_ii/apost_exhortations/documents/hf_jp-ii_exh_22011999_ecclesia-in-america_en.html (accessed June 1, 2007).

———. 1998. *Fides et Ratio.* Vatican Translation. Boston: Pauline Books & Media.

———. 1998. "John Paul II on the American Experiment." *First Things* 82: 36–37.

———. 1995. *Evangelium Vitae.* Vatican Translation. Boston: Pauline Books & Media.

———. 1994. Letter to Families. Vatican Website: http://www.vatican.va/holy_father/john_paul_ii/letters/documents/hf_jp-ii_let_02021994_families_en.html (accessed 19 January 2008).

———. 1993. *Veritatis Splendor.* Vatican Translation. Boston: Pauline Books & Media.

———. 1991. *Centesimus Annus.* Vatican Translation. Boston: St. Paul Books & Media.

———. 1987. *Solicitudo Rei Socialis.* Vatican Translation. Boston: Pauline Books & Media.

———. 1981. *Laborem Exercens.* Vatican Translation from Vatican Polyglot Press. Boston: Pauline Books & Media.

———. 1981. *Familiaris Consortio.* Vatican Translation. Boston: Pauline Books & Media.

———. 1979. *Redemptor Hominis.* Vatican Website: http://www.vatican.va/holy_father/john_paul_ii/encyclicals/documents/hf_jp-ii_enc_04031979_redemptor-hominis_en.html (accessed 19 January 2008).

Kennington, Richard. 2004. *On Modern Origins: Essays in Early Modern Philosophy*. Edited by Pamela Kraus and Frank Hunt. Lanham, Md.: Lexington Books.

Kurland, Philip B., and Ralph Lerner, eds. 1987. *The Founders' Constitution*. Vol. 1: *Major Themes*. Chicago: University of Chicago Press.

Kwitny, Jonathan. 1997. *Man of the Century: The Life and Times of John Paul II*. New York: Henry Holt.

Lawler, Peter Augustine, and Robert Martin Schaefer, eds. 2001. *American Political Rhetoric*, 4th ed. Lanham, Md.: Rowman & Littlefield.

"The Legacy of a Pope Who Changed History." 2005. *Economist*, 2 April: 1.

Locke, John. 1963. *Two Treatises of Government*. Edited by Peter Laslett. New York: New American Library.

Machiavelli, Niccolo. 1980. *The Prince*. Translated by Leo Paul S. de Alvarez. Prospect Heights, Ill.: Waveland Press.

Madison, James. 1975. *The Papers of James Madison*. Vol. 9. Edited by Robert A. Rutland. Chicago: University of Chicago Press.

"A Man for All Seasons." 2005. *Wall Street Journal*, 4 April: sec. A, p. 14.

May, Herber G., and Bruce M. Metzger, eds. 1973. *The New Oxford Annotated Bible with the Apocrypha*. New York: Oxford University Press. [RSV]

Mill, John Stuart. 1978. *On Liberty*. Indianapolis: Hackett.

Nietzsche, Friedrich. 1966. *Beyond Good and Evil: Prelude to a Philosophy of the Future*. Translated by Walter Kaufmann. New York: Vintage Books.

Novak, Michael. 2005 "John Paul the Great." *National Review*, 25 April: 32–36.

Percy, Walker. 1991. *Signposts in a Strange Land*. New York: Farrar, Straus, & Giroux.

Plato. 1968. *The Republic of Plato*. Translated by Allan Bloom. New York: Basic Books.

"Pope John Paul II: Keeper of the Flock for a Quarter of a Century." 2005. *The New York Times*, 3 April: sec. 1, p. 46.

Ratzinger, Joseph and Marcello Pera. 2006. *Without Roots: The West, Relativism, Christianity, Islam*. Translated by Michael F. Moore. New York: Basic Books.

Rossum, Ralph A., and G. Alan Tarr. *American Constitutional Law.* Vol. 1: *The Structure of Government*, 5th ed. New York: St. Martin's/Worth.

Sandoz, Eillis, ed. 1998. *Political Sermons of the Founding Era*, vol. 1. Indianapolis: Liberty Fund.

Shakespeare, William. 1976. *Coriolanus.* Edited by Philip Brockbank. New York: Routledge.

Stephen, Sir Leslie. 1961. *Hobbes.* Ann Arbor: University of Michigan Press.

Storing, Herbert J. 1995. *Toward a More Perfect Union.* Edited by Joseph M. Bessette. Washington: The AEI Press.

Strauss, Leo. 1953. *Natural Right and History.* Chicago: University of Chicago Press.

Suro, Roberto. 1987. "Pope, in Chile Protest Center, Hears Cry Against Terror." *The New York Times*, 6 April: sec A, p. 3.

Tarcov, Nathan. 1984. *Locke's Education for Liberty.* Chicago: University of Chicago Press.

Tocqueville, Alexis de. 2000. *Democracy in America.* Translated by Harvey Mansfield and Delba Winthrop. Chicago: University of Chicago Press.

Waldron, Jeremy. 2002. *God, Locke, and Equality: Christian Foundations of John Locke's Political Thought.* New York: Cambridge University Press.

Washington, George. 1988. *George Washington: A Collection.* Edited by William B. Allen. Indianapolis: Liberty Fund.

Weigel, George. 2005. "Mourning and Remembrance." *Wall Street Journal*, 4 April: sec. A, p. 14.

———. 2003. *The Final Revolution: The Resistance Church and the Fall of Communism.* New York: Oxford University Press.

———. 1999. *Witness to Hope: The Biography of John Paul II.* New York: Cliff Street Books.

Wilson, James. 1967. *The Works of James Wilson*, vol. 2. Edited by Robert Green McCloskey. Cambridge, Mass.: The Belknap Press of Harvard University Press.

Winters, Michael Sean. 2005. "After John Paul II: History Test." *The New Republic*, 18 April: 17.

INDEX